The Divine Feminine

A Reflective Spiritual Journey

By Dr. Al Carden, D.Min.

References

Melchizedek: "Our Gracious King-Priesthood in Christ by John L. Mastrogiovanni, D.Min. All rights reserved. No part of this book may be reproduced in any form without written permission from the author. Copyrighted in 2013. Used by permission from the author.

The Amplified Bible text may be quoted and/or reprinted up to and inclusive of one thousand (1,000) verses without express written permission of the Publisher providing the verses do not amount to a complete book of the Bible nor do the verses quoted account for 50% of the total work in which they are quoted.

Scripture quotations marked (KJV) or unmarked are taken from the King James Version.

THE MIRROR: The Bible translation from the original text and paraphrased in contemporary speech with commentary by Francois du Toit. Scripture taken from THE MIRROR. Copyrighted 2012. Used by permission of The Author.

Dictionary definitions themselves are not copyrightable unless they are particularly creative/original, because only original works can be copyrighted...and definitions for most words have not changed much since 1923 placing them in the public domain.

BORN FROM ABOVE—What Jesus Really Said: All rights reserved. No part of this book may be used or reproduced in any manner without the written permission from the author except in the case of brief quotations embodied in critical articles and reviews.

This edition published 2025
Copyright @ 2025 by Alan Carden
www.bridgebuilder101.com

Table of Contents

References	2
Introduction	5
The Divine Feminine	6
Remember	8
In Rememberance	10
Walking in the Dark	12
The Seemingly insignificant	14
The Rock	16
The Revelation of Eve	18
The Return	20
The Outward Appearance	22
The Numinous	24
The Mirror	26
The Journey of Grief	28
The Harvest	31
The Embrace	34
The Ego	36
The Cost of Distractions	38
The Cemetry	40
The Builder's heart	42
Showing Up	45
Recognition	47
Paradox	49
No 23	51
Moving Out	54
Love	57
Letting Go	60
Kinsman Redeemer	62
Judgement	64
Joy comes in the morning	66
Imagination	68
I Can See	70
Humility	72
Green Light	74
Fear	76
Face to Face	78
Ears to Hear	80
Deja Vu	82
Condemnation	84
Competition?	86

Table of Contents

Born Again 88
Being Spirit 90
Behold the Lamb 92
Behold his Face 95
Bad Theology 96
Angels Unaware 98
Calamities and Destructive Storms 101
Unbelief 103
Non Violence 105
Vibrations 107
The Yolk 109
The Revelation 111
The Light Seed 114
Believing is Seeing 116

Introduction

I am truly honored to be the scribe for this project. When I received the awareness of how the Divine Feminine, also known as the Holy Spirit, was unknown within the lives of so many of Mother/Father God's children here on school room earth, it became clear that the Spirit's presence needed to be unveiled. It's not that she is not present, but if her presence is ignored or excused by the masculine energy within humanity, the amazing gifts of her presence will continue to be forfeited. When this happens, there is an imbalance that lowers humanity's spiritual vibrations, best described by a desire to be in control. It does not matter if one is male or female for such control issues to surface.

The Divine Feminine is best recognized by compassion, mercy, grace, kindness, forgiveness, and of course, Love. These attributes are present within humility. Self-exaltation creates the barrier that pushes the Divine Feminine away, allowing the ego to make selfish decisions. When such decisions are made while the Divine Feminine is consciously or unconsciously ignored, it causes all kinds of issues to surface related to control, hatred, belittlement, disease, violence, evil, and premature physical death.

In this project, there are fifty-two reflections that offer encouragement to the reader. It is recommended that a reflection be read and used for meditation on a weekly basis. It is my prayer and desire that while embarking on this reflective journey, the reader will become increasingly aware of the Divine Feminine and her amazing presence. Once the Divine Masculine and Divine Feminine are balanced within our awareness, the possibilities that will embrace our understanding will cause a spiritual ripple effect increasing our Light vibration. We all are Mother/Father God's divine offspring. It is my hope that these reflections will be shared with friends and family so they too, will reap the blessings of Mother/Father God.

Blessings on your journey,

Dr. Al Carden, D.Min.

The Divine Feminine

This reflection is very important to grasp because of what is being held up for the reader to consider. As human beings, the reality of masculinity and femininity has been part and parcel of our existence. On a physical level, both male and female are needed for physical life, as we know it, to thrive and continue. Of course, this is not anything that we as humans are not already aware of. What is being held up in this reflection, pertains to the idea that as human beings, we have both masculine and feminine energies within us. These energies aid humanity to better understand one another.

To not be aware of both energies functioning within the human frame, is to disregard the energy that does not pertain to our physical sexual identity. For instance, when men are unaware of the feminine energy that exists within them, this will cause issues of control over females seeing them, in their mind, as weak. When this kind of thinking surfaces within the masculine energy, a rapid loss of balance occurs, and the female can quickly become the victim of this imbalance in emotional, mental, and physical ways. Since the male physical body tends to be stronger than the female physical body, often the absence of the awareness of the feminine energy within the male can cause the utilization of their physical strength to overpower the female. This often surfaces with issues of physical and mental abuse that may relate to shame, fear, anger, and internal pain from prior situations heaped upon the male child. Unfortunately, this kind of abuse can originate from both male and female.

Please consider the idea that masculine and feminine energies, that exist within us, must be balanced for love and care of the other to take precedence. The success of our ability to love the other will determine what each energy brings to the process. Hopefully we have entertained the idea of the difference between head and heart knowledge. Both head and heart knowledge are necessary for balance to be recognized. If the feminine energy is predominate, then the awareness of boundaries that are like guardrails to protect the traveler, may not be noticed and may cause the recipient to trust in those who want to take advantage causing destruction of the innocent. In such a situation, the masculine energy that is balanced with the feminine, will step up to protect the innocent traveler allowing the compassion brought by the feminine, to continue to teach.

This reflection is being shared in hopes that humanity will call out to the Divine Feminine and the Divine Masculine, recognizing that both are eternally balanced within Source, so that this balance will take precedence within our earthly human frame. They are never out of balance within the heavenly realm. However, they can become imbalanced within humanity here on school room earth for the purpose of aiding our growth and decisions to choose Love over fear. It is being held up for you to consider that the Holy Spirit is the Divine Feminine. That is based on the feminine Hebrew word for wind, "Ruach" pronounced (ru-ock) that identified the Spirit that hovered over our chaos as described in the Genesis account of creation in the bible. When one becomes aware of this Divine Wind that dwells within each of us, that is when the chaos of not knowing who and whose we are is blown away.

Remember

As I have aged it has become apparent that there are just some things I don't remember. Even when my friends and family tell what they recall about a certain event, of which I was a part, I still have trouble remembering it. And of course, they look at me like I have lost all my marbles. That is not to say that I don't remember most stuff but there are some things that seem to escape my memory.

Have you ever thought about the word remember? We use this term probably more than we realize. "Hey! do you remember what she said last week?" "Do you remember what pair of shoes I wore with this outfit last time?" I'm sure if you thought about it, you would agree that remembering is something we do often without even giving it much thought.

As I have pondered this word, I decided to look up the first part of the word remember or the "re" part of the word to see what the dictionary said about it. This is what I found, "a prefix, occurring originally in loanwords from Latin, used with the meaning 'again' or 'again and again' to indicate repetition, or with the meaning 'back' or 'backwards' to indicate withdrawal or backward motion." What this amounts to, at least in my understanding, pertains to the idea that to re-member would suggest that one would be brought back to their original condition. Take the word return for instance. To re-turn would suggest that one had to have turned away from their original path and by returning they would in essence come back to their origin or beginning.

In my personal studies I have come to a certain awareness of the term "remember." In this reflection I would like to share how my new understanding of this term has opened an amazing thought process of which I am eager to share with you.

The night that Jesus shared the Passover meal with his disciples just before his crucifixion, he is recorded as saying, "...do this in remembrance of me." Now we could say that Jesus just wanted his disciples to remember him as a friend who had fellowshipped with them for some three years and when they broke the bread and drank from the cup, they would have fond memories of those times spent together. Or maybe to re-member him meant something much deeper and more profound. I would suggest that Jesus wasn't indicating an earthly remembrance of himself to his twelve disciples.

Is it possible that what Jesus wanted us to remember was our origin in Source or to put it another way, to awaken to our true design? After all, it is reported that Jesus said, "If you have seen me, you have seen the Father." As I have reflected on this repeatedly, it has assisted me to hear how "remember" has been used in other ways. For instance, let's say you had joined a particular organization becoming a member in good standing. For some reason you decided to leave that organization due to some misunderstandings. Years had gone by and the memory of the good times you experienced in that fellowship continued to surface in your thoughts. One day, you received a phone call from one of the members of that organization inviting you to join an upcoming meeting. You decided to accept the invitation. While you were at the meeting, you were invited to return and rejoin the organization asking for your forgiveness for the misunderstandings that caused you to leave in the first place. You began to feel the love you had experienced while being a member years ago. Suddenly, the organization remembered you into their group. Remembering is very important to who we are. To not remember may also be helpful depending upon the circumstances.

For God to choose not to remember our sins, would mean that he simply separated us from our sins and does not reattach them to us. I believe the scriptures indicate that God removes our transgressions from us as far as the east is from the west. So, if Jesus wanted each of us to "re-member" him then perhaps it stands to reason that we were and are originally attached to him in our beginning because all things exist and consist in the Christ energy. The Christ energy is the heart of the Creator. In Source we breathe and move and have our being. What I have found so intriguing about remembering is the idea that sin does not separate us from God. For Jesus to invite us to remember him is an indicator of our original and eternal attachment to him for you cannot remember unless you were a member once.

In Rememberance

There is a rather mysterious character mentioned in the Old Testament of the Bible. He is introduced in the book of Genesis chapter fourteen. His name is Melchizedek. He is identified as the King of Salem later called Jerusalem. He is also identified as the King Priest of God Most High. What is so fascinating about this King-Priest is what he brings to Abram, later called Abraham, after he has defeated the kings of Sodom and Gomorrah in battle returning his captured nephew Lot and his possessions. What he brings to Abram is a distant reminder of what Jesus of Nazareth highlighted at the Passover meal just before his crucifixion namely, bread and wine.

According to John Mastrogiovanni in his book Melchizedek, Our Gracious King Priesthood in Christ, "The Melchizedekian king-priest order is like no other priesthood in the known world. Whether Aaronic/Levitical or pagan, the Melchizedekian order stands in a place all by itself. The crucial element of its priesthood is that it brings a revelation of the Divine through a Living Temple" This Living Temple is the dwelling place of the Holy Spirit and where the presence of God Most High abides of which Melchizedek is the king-priest. "used by permission".

What I hold up for the reader to consider is centered around the bread and wine Melchizedek brought to Abram. I don't think it was a coincidence that Jesus highlighted bread and wine indicating what it represented to and for his disciples. It is recorded in the Gospels, Jesus showing that the bread represented his body that is broken for you and the wine represented his blood that was shed for you. All this was done before his disciples really understood just what was going to happen that fateful night in the breaking of the bread (the crucifixion) including the shedding of the blood of Christ (the wine).

It is recorded in the gospel of Luke chapter 22 and verse 19 of the Amplified Bible that Jesus took a loaf of bread and after giving thanks broke it and gave it to them saying, "This is my body which is given for you; do this in remembrance of me." Much earlier during his ministry Jesus had indicated that he was the Bread of Life. Several places in scripture reveal how bread is synonymous with Life.

Regarding wine, there are places in scripture that highlight the essentialness of wine's spiritual necessity because it comes from the Vine (John 15) of which we all are branches. One such example is the wedding feast at Cana where Jesus turns water into wine. This being the first reported miracle Jesus performs, is it possible that wine would play a significant role particularly when one considers that Melchizedek brought wine as one of the components of the priestly function of God Most High to Abram?

Anyone can enter a local grocery store that sells bread and wine. One can pass by the shelves where the numerous loaves of bread are on display for purchase never giving any thought to what the bread represents. Likewise, one can walk past the numerous bottles of wine displayed on the grocery store shelves never giving any thought to what the wine represents. This reflection holds up for us a challenge that is based on remembrance. The church likes to highlight communion services consecrating certain types of bread and wine to make that service official. But consider that the most important aspect of the bread and wine, no matter where it is encountered, opens the door for our remembrance of Mother/Father God Most High in the Christ energy revealed by Jesus! This awareness places each of us within the same priestly order as Melchizedek. This priestly order has ministry to all as the very key to our existence and this ministry is driven by the Divine Feminine in balance with the Divine Masculine which is Love. "In remembrance" would not be possible unless we were already acquainted and familiar with the Christ energy. Otherwise, Peter would not have had the insight to tell Jesus that Jesus was the Christ, the Son of the Living God.

Walking in the Dark

This reflection regards what it means to be walking in the dark. To walk a path that is undetectable doesn't really make a lot of sense. Yet in a manner of speaking, many people walk a path that is filled with fear and uncertainty. Uncertainty about the path they're on, where this path leads are but a couple of anxieties that present themselves to the traveler. But even though they are presented, the traveler may not recognize such anxieties because they are distracted due to their earthly pursuits. Those who have awakened to the dark path on which they have walked, testify to such anxieties that before the awakening was not recognized.

This reflection holds up for the reader to consider that darkness may be the absence of light or it may be ignorance of the light's presence. If one were not aware of the spiritual light that dwells within them, then it would make sense for them to say that there is no spiritual light in them. Obviously, the light being spoken of is not visible light but rather more inclined to understanding or awareness.

No-one can convince anyone that such Light exists on the physical plane. It is not seen with the naked eye. Rather, it is experienced within the soul and psyche of humanity. When this Light has yet to be experienced, then all sorts of substitutes seek to fill the void, and this is all based on belief. Usually what fills the void is what the naked eye sees. The Source of this Light is Spirit and Love which is the Divine Feminine of Source. When this Light has yet to be noticed, then as humans, we seek to fill the void with what the world has to offer. The unfortunate disadvantage of such human activities places them in seeking reliance on things and status.

The more the ignorance of the Light prevails, the more the desire for worldly possessions increase. Attached to such desire includes envy, covetousness, and wanting what others possess. If one does not have the wherewithal to obtain these possessions, then stealing may be considered. This desire for things increases exponentially and once their obtaining has been successful, then defending their possessions takes center stage which may include violence. All the while the Light that dwells within them has been ignored and the path they continue to walk is in spiritual darkness.

The scriptures indicate that men love darkness rather than light because their deeds are evil. Iris Lohrengel, in her book Born From Above, What Jesus Really Said explains it like this: "Not recognizing the light results in 'condemnation' in Greek krisis. The principal meaning of krisis is "separation" but it also means, depending on the context, 'giving an opinion, making a decision or judgement.' 'Condemnation' is the result of our separation from God, separation not in the sense of being disobedient or rebellious, but separation in the sense of believing oneself to be separate individuals who exists independently from and outside of God."

When one is not aware of the Spiritual Light that dwells within them, then they can rest assured that their life is full of condemnation, judgement and darkness. They may not even be aware of their predicament because their attention has become focused on their greed, selfishness and worldly possessions. Until they encounter an unexpected situation that completely overwhelms them spiritually, they will be blind to it. In this world we are tested by fear. The only way one will become aware of the Love that casts out fear is to experience fear. It is not pleasant. As a matter of fact, it is horrendous. So if one finds themselves in a situation that is so fearfully overwhelming, call out to the Source of Love and in so doing, that Love will rescue them from fear and the Spiritual awakening will have opened the spiritual eyes of the blind.

The Seemingly Insignificant

Is it just my imagination or does it seem that insignificant things in life are not insignificant at all? You may think this is an odd question but allow this reflection to hold up some things offered in scripture that just may dispel or better, may reveal something that if overlooked, could get in the way of our life-purpose while we exist on school room earth.

Jesus makes it a priority to emphasize the importance of the seemingly insignificant. Here is an example. While Jesus went about ministering to all kinds of people, he tended to minister to those to whom the religious of his day had neglected or ignored. He ate with tax collectors and prostitutes and would regularly receive criticism from religious leaders for his actions.

Another example was the encounter Jesus had with the Samaritan woman at Jacob's well recorded in the gospel of John chapter four. The religious leaders looked down their noses at the Samaritans considering them to be second class citizens or worse. There are religions that treat women as second-class citizens too. Any time the masculine energy within each of us overshadows the feminine energy that we all possess, then the important aspects of love, compassion, caring, and giving, based upon the need to lift the other is ignored and as a result our ego or physical self, causes our spiritual vibration to lessen. When our vibration lessens, darkness, related to greed, selfishness, hatred, based upon our desire to exalt ourselves over the other takes control.

Additionally, Jesus' encounter with Zacchaeus, who was a tax collector, had climbed a sycamore tree to see Jesus as he passed on the road. It is not so much that these tax collectors were insignificant, but their seemingly insignificance was created by those whose opinions carried much weight within the religious community.

While meditating on these ideas, the parable of the mustard seed came to mind. As I gave thought to what I had been taught regarding the mustard seed, suddenly, the seemingly insignificance of this very small seed surfaced. Despite the seed's size, once planted, produces one of the largest plants in the garden. You can find this example in the gospel of Matthew 13:31-32. So, in essence, maybe size does matter.

The significance of this insignificant seed, once planted and fully matured, becomes one of the largest herbs in the garden resembling a tree. The benefits of such a tree like herb has branches where birds can perch. It also offers shade for those needing to find a cool place to rest in the heat of the day. If the farmer chose not to plant this seed due to its small insignificant size, thinking that what it may produce will also be insignificant, then the potential hidden within its seeming insignificance would never be discovered.

If we project our opinions of others based upon how we view them, their lifestyle, their outward appearance, their economic status, their education, their behaviors, their culture, that may be different from our own, we run the risk of lumping these children of Mother/Father God into judgmental categories whereby we simply turn our backs on them and walk away.

It does not take a rocket scientist to discover how people of privilege continue to seek ways of distancing themselves from those to whom they have judged insignificant. What I hold up for those reading this entry and myself to consider is to be aware of the importance of the insignificant. If we as human beings begin to recognize our value based on where we came from and to whom we belong, we just may begin to see the value in everyone we meet. We are spirit beings made of Love. It makes a big difference when we recognize our Source, and we make the decision to reflect Love's Source to everyone.

The Rock

In chapter twenty of the book of Numbers in the Old Testament of the bible there is recorded a story about the children of Israel. It seems they were dissatisfied with their leaders, namely Moses and his brother Aaron. Their complaint included their dissatisfaction with their present location. As they described their whereabouts, they raised the fact that Moses had led them out of Egypt, where they had food to eat and water to drink for themselves as well as their livestock. Now they did not have those precious items. The more they contended with Moses and Aaron about their situation the more hurtful their insinuations became. They even wished they had died along with their brethren during the plague before leaving Egypt.

So, Moses and Aaron fall on their faces before God in the Tent of Meetings to find out what to do next. As the story goes, the Glory of the Lord came upon them instructing Moses to take his rod and go before the assembly to a particular Rock. They are instructed to "speak" to the Rock to give forth its water. This was to be done in the presence of the congregation.

Due to the anger kindled by Moses after hearing the contention of the congregation of Israel, Moses choses to strike the Rock rather than speaking to it. This reflection is centered around Mother/Father God's response to humanity's anger. The apostle Paul reiterated in I Corinthians chapter ten that all of Israel were under the cloud and passed through the sea. They all ate the same spiritual meat and drank the same spiritual drink; for they drank of that spiritual Rock and that Rock was the Christ energy which is the heart of Mother/Father God.

What I hold up for the reader to consider pertains to the response of Source despite the anger of Moses. According to the story, Moses was instructed to speak to the Rock and out of this Rock would flow water enough to satisfy the thirst of the entire Israelite congregation including their livestock. Sometimes humanity's anger can get the best of us. I'm not saying that anger is a bad thing. The scriptures indicate to be angry and sin not. So, Moses takes his rod and strikes the Rock twice. Despite his disobedience, water flows out of the Rock.

What does this mean? Good question. Here are a few thoughts to ponder. Mother/Father God does not respond to mankind's anger the way mankind responds to his or her own anger. Usually when someone makes us angry, we tend to reflect their anger back to them in retaliation. Despite the anger of Moses, water flowed from the Rock showing God's compassion rather than condemnation. If we take the apostle Paul's comparison of the Rock being the Christ energy to heart, then it becomes clear when Jesus tells the Samaritan woman at the well that if she knew who it was that was asking her for a drink, she would have asked him, and he would have given her living water. Or as it is recorded in John chapter seven and verse thirty-seven, Jesus stood and cried saying, "If any man thirst, let him come unto me and drink.

"Finally, when Jesus was crucified, the Roman guard present there took a spear piercing the side of Jesus rather than breaking his legs. It is recorded that from his pierced side flowed a combination of blood and water. This may indicate the possibility that Jesus may not have been clinically dead for the blood and water to flow out of his body his heart had to be beating.

Mother/Father God's love for each of us surpasses our anger and the decisions we make because of it. God's mercy and grace also surpass our anger in such a way that if we will venture to let our anger go while desiring to embrace Mother/Father God's surpassing love, the water that flowed from the Rock of which you have been invited to drink, will indeed spring up from within you satisfying your spiritual thirst. I suppose there is only one way to find out if what is being suggested is true…

The Revelation of Eve

So as the creation story goes, God declared that it was not suitable for Adam to be alone. The scriptures indicate that God crafted out of the same soil of which he made Adam every bird and wild animal bringing them to Adam to see what he would call them. After he has given them all names, Adam realized that none of the birds or wild beasts were suitable to be his helper. I'm thinking that perhaps this was because none of the animals or birds looked like Adam or functioned like he did physically or emotionally. Now this is where the story begins to get interesting. Once God causes Adam to fall into a deep sleep a rib is taken from him. Out of this rib God fashions a helper. Once Adam sees Eve, Genesis 2:23 in the Amplified Bible records him as saying, "Then Adam said, this is now bone of my bones and flesh of my flesh …"

This reflection centers around the idea that Eve was present within Adam at his creation with the notion that it was just a matter of time before she would be revealed. As I have given this idea much thought, I draw your attention to the conversations recorded in Genesis chapter three first between the serpent and Eve and then between Adam, Eve and God. It is interesting to note that the serpent did not have anything to say once the voice of God came calling in the garden. After the garden couple partake of the forbidden fruit the scripture records "their eyes were open" and they realized they were naked.

As the meeting between God, Adam, Eve, and the serpent continues, a very interesting encounter occurs. A recent rendition or explanation of this encounter told by Paul Young, the author of The Shack, goes something like this. It is recorded that before Eve was taken from Adam, his task was to "keep" the garden. The word "keep" when used as a noun, is defined as the innermost and strongest structure or central tower of a medieval castle. In other words, when under attack by an enemy this innermost structure was to be kept from invasion at all costs. Then it stands to reason to ask the following question. Where was the serpent when he is revealed in the creation story? You got it! The serpent was IN the garden. In other words, Adam did not keep it and allowed the enemy to invade. Remember, this was before Eve was taken from Adam's side. The only other time the word "keep" is used in the creation story is when Adam is expelled from the garden and Eve follows him out and an angel with a flaming sword is placed at the entrance to "keep" the garden.

The conversation between God, Adam and Eve continues and God asks Adam what happened. The way Paul Young tells it, Adam walks over to stand beside the serpent and then points his finger at his mate and exclaims to God, "...that woman you gave me! It's her fault!" Then God asks Eve what she did. She answers, "...the serpent thoroughly deceived me, and I ate." The next focused comment from God reveals a truth that if one is observant will see it portrayed in everyday life. Picture this. God looks at Adam and says, gesturing to Eve, "through her you will be saved." Then God points his finger at the serpent and says to it gesturing to Eve, "...and through her you will be destroyed."

It is recorded in Genesis 3:15 that God placed enmity between the seed of the serpent and the seed of the woman. Enmity is defined as a feeling or condition of hostility, hatred, ill will, animosity, or antagonism. What I hold up for us to consider in this reflection is related to the absolute value God placed in the woman Eve before she was ever taken out of the side of Adam. It was as though she was hidden within him until she was needed to assist in the salvation of Adam or mankind. It is suggested that since Adam did not keep the garden that perhaps he had already allied with the serpent before Eve was revealed. God knew beforehand that it was going to be through the woman that mankind would realize salvation. If you think about it, a lot of the major religions of the world treat woman as second-class citizens or worse. Even in religions claiming to be Christian also behave in like manner. I would suggest that their treatment is an outward expression of the enmity between her and her enemy.

Finally, what I have decided to be on the lookout for in today's religious circles includes the subtle ways men seek to put down, discourage, reduce, control, contrive or any other description of woman's belittlement to be just what it is, the hiss of the serpent!!!!

The Return

Looking up the definition of prodigal in *Dictionary.com*, the definition read, "wastefully or recklessly extravagant." The definition of extravagant read, "spending much more than is necessary or wise; wasteful." Recently, a meditation on the parable of the prodigal son recorded in the gospel of Luke chapter fifteen, revealed a discovery. The discovery was right in plain sight. Yet for the meditator, the question was asked, "why haven't you seen this before?" Then it was remembered that most of the discoveries made in the past were truths that were staring the meditator right in the face as if they were waiting to be discovered when the time was right.

I have heard many a sermon on the prodigal son. This reflection, however, is not about the sermons previously heard. What I hold up for consideration pertains to what draws us. If you are not familiar with this story, I invite you to find where it is recorded in scripture and become familiar with the journey of this young man after he leaves home to venture into a foreign land. Let's say you were the parent of two sons, and your youngest son asked you to give him the portion of the family inheritance that would eventually come to him. What would you do? Let's say you gave him his portion of the inheritance.

"So, this young inexperienced son takes his newly acquired inheritance, packs his belongings and heads to a place he has never been before". As long as his inheritance remains intact, he is able to enjoy living life while experiencing things totally foreign to him. Soon his inheritance is gone and the rich lifestyle he had been experiencing has disappeared. The scripture indicates this young son wasted his inheritance on riotous living. And if matters could not get worse, a famine strikes the land, and this young son becomes overwhelmingly in need of the very basics of life like food and shelter.

I recall hearing an interpretation of this parable. The interpreter indicated that the young son was Jesus, and the earth was the foreign land and somehow Jesus' resurrection was how the parable ended as Jesus goes back to his father. I don't agree. What I hold up for us to consider is that we, you and I, are the young prodigal son in this story. As I consider the mistakes I have made and how much I have stumbled throughout my life, it is not difficult to identify with this young son who was bent on having his own way. My extravagance, not just in physical ways but in selfish egocentric ways, has forced me to be taught by my misfortunes.

What occurred within the mind of this wayward son will eventually occur to each of us. It is a coming to one's senses and changing one's mind that becomes necessary to awaken us to who we really are. This wayward son, while seated in a pigpen, is so hungry he is tempted to eat the slop meant for the pigs. His mind recalls his father's house and the fact that even his father's servants have enough to eat. So, he devises a plan to go back to his father's house but not as a son but rather as a servant. It dawned on me that this wayward son has lost sight of who he really is. He now compromises his identity based on his riotous living in that foreign land.

So, he gets up and begins to make his way back to his father's house. What he does not consider however is his father's love for him. It is very easy to allow our bad choices to distract us from the truth of who we really are. You see, the fact that he was headed to his father's house reveals that he was returning to where he began. This is a journey we all will make. Once we make that transition through death of the body, we begin to be drawn toward our Father's house. We may even have some idea that perhaps due to the egocentric choices we have made in this life, we would settle for being a servant. What we may not have considered is the Love our Mother/Father God has for us. Can you imagine thinking that you are no longer a son or daughter of the Highest, based upon your earthly behavioral choices. As we seek to compromise our identity to be less than who we really are, we are greeted and welcomed into the very presence of Source where the celebration of our return is well under way. Please understand that to "re-turn" we must remember our first turning away from where we originated. Our consent to come to school room earth was for our need to learn and grow spiritually. If you had to answer the question, ("what have you learned during your lifetime on planet earth?") how you would answer the question will determine your awareness. What do you think the prodigal learned?

We are children of Mother/Father God. Our behaviors here cannot change our genesis nor our Source's Love for us. When we awaken to our sonship or daughtership in the Christ energy Jesus came to reveal within each of us and realize that ALL has been forgiven through the shedding of blood of Jesus Christ, then "the return" to our Father's House becomes the journey to celebration!

The Outward Appearance

What is being held up for your consideration, pertains to how we as human beings see one another. There is an interesting account of the prophet Samuel being sent to Bethlehem to anoint a new king of Israel due to the present king's disobedience. We know this new king to be David the son of Jesse the Bethlehemite. This account if found in the Old Testament in I Samuel chapter 16.

Samuel did not know which son of Jesse he was supposed to anoint as king. The message Mother/Father God gave to him was that He would let him know which of Jesse's sons he was supposed to anoint. Jesse had eight sons. When the eldest son passed before Samuel, he thought to himself, surely the Lord would anoint the oldest son, but what is recorded in the seventh verse in the Amplified Bible concerning this account is being held up for your consideration. It reads:

"But the Lord said to Samuel, do not look at his appearance or the height of his stature, for I have rejected him. For the Lord sees not as man sees; for man looks on the outward appearance, but the Lord looks on the heart."

After the first seven sons of Jesse have passed before Samuel realizing that none of these sons are to be anointed king, he asks if there are any more. Jesse indicates that the youngest son is keeping the sheep. Keeping the sheep is the task of a shepherd. The shepherd, if their task is taken seriously, puts the sheep and their safety first before themselves. Leadership then must be about putting others before yourself.

When Peter, the disciple of Jesus, had denied knowing Jesus three times, Jesus is recorded to have asked Peter three times if he loved him. Each time Peter answered that he did love him, Jesus said, "If you love me then feed my sheep." The word "pastor" derives from the Latin noun pastor which means shepherd. The shepherd leads his or her sheep to pasture, to set to grazing, to cause to eat.

So how do we see one another? Would it be possible to see ourselves as sheep? After all it is recorded in Isaiah 53:6 the following:

All we like sheep have gone astray. We have turned, everyone, to his own way, and the Lord has made to light on Him the guilt and iniquity of us all."

You mean to tell me that no matter who I see, no matter what others look like, they are like sheep having gone astray? Does that include race, culture, language, and any other differences that are unlike my own? Yes, and that means I have gone astray as well.

Racism has dominated our world to such a degree that we as human beings continue to be blind because we would rather look on the outward appearance rather than to look on the heart of others. Due to our past behaviors, there is a lot of pain and suffering that we have experienced. We would rather hold grudges toward those who have hurt us placing ourselves in self-made prisons being overcome by anger seeking ways to retaliate. But you might say, "but I'm not God, only God looks on the heart." It also says in Matthew 19:26, "… but with God all things are possible."

How we see one another depends first and foremost with our relationship with Mother/Father God and the Christ energy that's already within us that Jesus came to teach. I really did not understand what such a relationship would cause until an awakening took place within me that frankly continues to surprise. I promise that when you choose to offer kindness in the face of disappointing behavioral circumstances and you practice this kindness consistently, The Mother/Father God of Love will bless you to bring much needed healing not only to the one to whom you show this kindness, but it will ripple outward to so many bringing peace and healing to you and everyone it touches as well.

The Numinous

This reflection centers around our ability to recognize and experience the numinous. Numinous describes the presence of a deity or spirit being. That should not be so surprising since all of us are spirit beings. The fact that we are made of God or Source is an indication that we have within us the wherewithal to recognize such a presence. You may say that you have never had such an experience and due to that, such a presence is only fictitious. Allow me to use a Star Wars quote that may aid us in grasping this spiritual awareness. The original Star Wars movie had Obi-Wan Kenobi encouraging Luke Skywalker to experience "the force" by "stretching out with his feelings" In other words, do not rely upon what you see with your physical eyes but rather trust that which you cannot see. The apostle Paul indicates in II Corinthian 5:7 that we walk by faith and not by sight.

The word "faith" contains an element of trust, but trust in what or who. Galatians chapter two and verse twenty of the New Testament holds a key element for your consideration as we continue to offer this reflection. The writer of Galatians indicates that we were crucified with Christ Jesus. Paul's understanding of this idea comes from his awareness that this Christ Jesus was revealed within him Galatians 1:15 - 16. Once this revelation came into view, Paul realized that to have Christ Jesus within him meant that whatever happened to Christ Jesus will eventually happen to all of us on a spiritual level. Once again Paul indicates that he was crucified with Christ. He communicated this while he was physically alive. The faith "of" the Son of God is very important to consider because it indicates that it is not our faith that we live by, but rather it is the ' faith of the Christ energy" that matters most.

The "faith" chapter in Scripture is found in Hebrews chapter eleven of the New Testament. In the King James Version the first verse reads, "Now faith is the substance of things hoped for, the evidence of things not seen." Allow me to encourage you to take the idea of living by the faith of the Son of God by substituting the name "Jesus" for the word "faith" in Hebrews eleven verse one. The first time I did it I was overwhelmed with the truth that surfaced in my thinking. It would read like this, "Now Jesus is the substance of things hoped for, the evidence of things not seen." In other words, Jesus is the visible representation of that which is unseen and so are we. Just because it is unseen with our physical eyes does not mean it does not exist. Most of the time we cannot see our breath, but we believe that our breath is present within us.

This brings us back to our original thought concerning the numinous. Jesus said that he would send the Holy Spirit to be our Comforter. Why would he describe the Holy Spirit as a comforter? Here is something to consider. Because the word Spirit comes from the Hebrew word Ruach meaning "wind" and this Hebrew word is feminine, the Comforter can easily be understood as the Divine Feminine Mother-God that brings compassion and love when those things are absent in various circumstances. The Divine Feminine is always present with the Divine Masculine and their balance always brings Light and Love. Another name for the Holy Spirit is Paraclete. This word suggests that the Holy Spirit comes alongside to give comfort and solace. The Spirit is always present. Allow me to encourage you, by the faith of the Son of God, that you consider trusting in that which you cannot see and in so doing you will stretch out with your feelings, so to speak, and begin the journey of walking by faith and not by sight. Once you engage this journey and you witness the Numinous presence of the Holy Spirit within, you will grasp a greater awareness of the Christ energy Jesus came to reveal.

The Mirror

This reflection centers around the idea of transformation. The online dictionary defines transformation as a change in form or appearance or nature or character. I suppose some transformations are subtle, meaning some changes occur without much recognition. I found this to be true with my waistline. One day as I was putting on a familiar pair of comfortable blue jeans suddenly, they were not as comfortable as I remembered. I guess this only proves that I need to stay on top of some transformations.

The transformation that is inspiring this reflection, however, has to do with a different kind of growth. I have been intrigued with the idea of the mirror image spoken of in the biblical passage found in James 1:23-25. Here is how it reads in the Mirror Bible,

"The difference between a mere spectator and a participator is that both of them hear the same voice and perceive in its message the face of their own genesis reflected as in a mirror; they realize that they are looking at themselves, but for the one it seems just too good to be true; this person departs **(back to the old way of seeing himself)** *and immediately forgets what manner of person he is; never giving another thought to the one he saw in the mirror. The other one is mesmerized by what he sees; captivated by the effect of a law that frees a person from the obligation to the old written code that restricted one to their own efforts and willpower. No distraction of contradiction can dim the impact of what is seen in the mirror concerning the law of perfect liberty* **(the law of faith)** *that now frees everyone to get on with the act of living the life* **(of their original design.)** *They find a new spontaneous lifestyle, the poetry of practical living. The law of perfect liberty is the image and likeness of God revealed in Christ, now redeemed in mankind as in a mirror."*

Over time, I have sought to wrap my mind around this contrasted idea between the spectator and the participator. As I began to examine their differences it became apparent to me that sometimes I was a participator but most of the time I was a spectator. In other words, I began to realize that as I peered into this mirror, all too often I would turn and walk away forgetting what I had beheld in the mirror. This became evident in my behaviors and particularly the kind of behaviors that distracted me from my relationship with Mother/Father God.

When I began to realize that the Christ energy in Jesus is the Mirror image of what Mother/Father God sees in you and me, my understanding started to open some. I came across another statement that aided me further, "…we do not grow more complete, rather we simply grow in the knowledge of our completeness." I was under the notion that somehow, I was not complete, and I needed to do something or strive to become something by acting a certain way that would make me more accepted by the Divine. Little did I know that I was already accepted within the Divine and this acceptance was not of my doing.

My awareness now is increasing. The importance of the mirror cannot be over emphasized. The "participator" continually looks into the mirror. Just recently I believe I heard the Divine Feminine, we call the Holy Spirit, speak a word to me that was so overwhelming concerning the mirror that it stopped me in my tracks, and I began weeping. What I heard was this, "Keep looking into the mirror until you see what I see." Do you ever wonder what Mother/Father God sees when looking at you? Just the fact that you and I exist lets me know that our Source purposed you and I and everyone else to be invited to look intently into that mirror. And if we purpose to look long enough, we will see the face of our genesis, our beginning in the Christ energy in Jesus, for He is the balanced mirror image of Mother/Father God. For Jesus said, "If you have seen me, you have seen the Father."

The Journey of Grief

This reflection is related to what it means to lose something of value. Anytime anyone loses anything of value, grief is the reaction. Elizabeth Kubler Ross was a psychiatrist working with mentally challenged patients. As she observed the reactions of her patients receiving bad news, with relationship to loss, she began to recognize from her patient's similar behaviors. The more she observed these similarities the more she began to understand an emerging pattern surfacing she called the process of grief. She wrote about her finding in her famous book On Death and Dying.

What she observed once someone received the bad news of loss, started out with what she termed "denial." Denial may be described as a numbing sensation that tends to set in to aid in coping with the trauma caused by the loss. It can be understood as the electrical service panel in your home or apartment. Once an electrical circuit is overloaded, the breaker in the electrical panel trips to keep the circuit from catching the house on fire. In other words, denial helps the individual cope with the trauma associated with the loss.

Secondly, once the denial begins to wear away and the numbing sensation decreases, then anger begins to set in. What was once unbelief, that the loss had occurred, was replaced by the fact that the loss happened and now anger fills what the denial had veiled over. This anger, depending on how severe the loss, heats up within a person's psyche causing such distress. When this anger reaches the boiling point, then the next stage in the grief process described by Ross is termed "bargaining."

Simply put, bargaining is looking for someone to blame for the loss. If someone very close to you is killed in an automobile accident and the person causing the accident was a drunk driver, more than likely your anger would soon turn to blaming the driver for their negligence in driving while intoxicated. It can get more complicated especially when it is not certain who was at fault for the loss. One might say, "If only the ambulance driver had gotten my mother to the hospital in time, she would still be alive. These and other statements are expressed to try and cope with losses. Often when we can't find anyone to blame, then our anger and blaming gets projected onto God.

These first three emotions, denial, anger, and bargaining tend to be relived over and over as we try to make sense of the loss we are experiencing. The result of not being able to come to any solution brings about the next stage in the grief process namely, "depression." Depression is that sinking feeling within us when we are no longer in control. There is a hopelessness that accompanies our inner being. We may try to hide it but most of the time it is very present. We may try to self-medicate this pain by overeating, taking drugs or consuming large amounts of alcohol to help us cope. Usually, these attempts to deal with the loss only complicate the process of reaching the last stage of Ross' grief process called "acceptance."

It has been said that grief work is the hardest work we will ever do in our lifetime. Grief work must be intentional. It is a good idea to take this grief journey with a trusted friend. For this journey to be successful in reaching acceptance, one can only get passed grief by going through it. In other words, you can't go over it or under it or around it, you must go through it to get past it. This means that to successfully get through grief, one must not run away from it.

Thoughts about the grief journey of various nations in our world also collectively go through this grief journey as well. It appears the denial of these various nations often ask themselves "is this really happening to us?" There are so many voices shouting out their pain to get the attention of those seemingly in control. The bargaining piece to these national grief processes seem to be coming from several different places. Everyone is pointing fingers. If these grief processes are accurate, national depression within these nations will certainly take its toll.

To reiterate, grief work is the hardest work we will ever do in our lifetime. Presently we are all asking "why" and "when" questions. Why is this happening? Why did we not see this coming? When will all of this go away? The "why" and "when" questions are always asked amid the grieving process. One of the evidences that we as human beings will approach the last stage of the grieving process, namely "acceptance" is when we start asking the "how" questions. In other words, how can we take what we are learning and apply it in the care of each other? How can we make room for all to be included? How can we become more loving toward one another? In essence, it is very important to usher the Divine Feminine back into our collective grief process. She never left but our recognition of what She brings is compassion and acceptance, which is the last stage of grief.

The scriptures indicate that humanity looks on the outward appearance, but Mother/Father God looks on the heart. The heart is the Christ energy Jesus came to earth to reveal. We can look on the heart as well because we come from Mother/Father God. We are the "Godkind." Because that is so, we come from Love. Once hope and prayer reveal acceptance, it will be surrounded and upheld in and by Love with the absolute absence of condemnation. We all are Loved and when we make that discovery and begin to show love to one another, the world will never be the same again!

he Harvest

There is a story recorded in Matthew's Gospel chapter thirteen verses 24 - 30 that speaks of a particular farmer that sowed wheat seeds in his field. As the story goes there was an enemy that came along during the night while the hired men were asleep and sowed thistles among the wheat. Once the wheat began to sprout so did the thistle. When it was discovered by the hired men that thistle was present among the wheat, they immediately asked the farmer as to how this happened. The farmer knew that the wheat seed that was planted was pure. His explanation? Some enemy did this. The farmhands suggested that they weed out the thistle to which the farmer replied, "No, if you weed out the thistles, you'll pull up the wheat, too. Let them grow together until harvest time. Then I will instruct the harvesters to pull up the thistles and tie them in bundles for the fire, then gather the wheat and put it in the barn."

This story has intrigued many for quite some time. I have heard various sermons preached using this text. I recall one sermon where the preacher used the text to indicate that the wheat represented the believers in Jesus and the thistles represented those who did not believe in Jesus. The fate of those who numbered with the thistles were bundled up and thrown in the fire. I must admit that by the time the sermon was finished and the alter call was extended to the congregation there were all kinds of people coming forward to seek assurance that they numbered among the wheat. When your theology is built on fear, much like the house built on the sand, there is no solid foundation. As I have given thought to what I witnessed that evening, I offer this reflection.

This reflection centers around personal insights that I continue to work on. This is a story told by Jesus. He seeks to bring understanding to those who are blind to what he is trying to get them to see. He doesn't automatically open their understanding and I think that is by design. I have become aware that when "night" or "darkness" is included in one of Jesus' stories it usually suggests that there is a lack of awareness on the part of those being told the story or those characters within the story, thus the darkness. Jesus is telling people what the kingdom of God is like not what it is.

I used to think the wheat in this story represented all of humanity. I continue to seek truth and recently an awareness came to me that I wish to share with you now. What if the field represents the physical human body and the thistles in the story represented "sin?" That leaves the wheat. The insight that came to me during a recent meditation leads me to consider that the wheat represents "the Love of God." I hold up for you to ponder that each one of us exists because we are made by and from LOVE. In essence, we are not only a thought of Mother/Father God we are the LOVE of Mother/Father God.

Source placed Love in a human body. We are spirit beings originating from LOVE and our spirit presence is what enters our human body before our physical birth. At some point in our human history, we began to believe a lie that we were less than the Love from whence we came. The lie, once internalized, veiled over the truth about ourselves and as a result, all kinds of base behaviors including fear, mistrust, envy, strife and murder escalated out of control. But Mother/Father God loved us so much that we were given numerous opportunities to learn the difference between love and fear so we would grow and mature spiritually for the good of all life.

As I have pondered this parable here are some additional thoughts. In Romans chapter seven the Apostle Paul gives his readers his own understanding regarding sin. In verses sixteen and seventeen he basically indicates that it is obvious that his conscience sides with the law which confirms then that it was not really himself that did these sinful things but "sin" that manifested its symptoms in him.

In Galatians chapter one and verse sixteen Paul indicates the following, "This is the heart of the gospel that I proclaim; it began with an unveiling of his Son in me ..." If the Apostle Paul discovered both "sin" and the "Son" in him, then I hold up for your consideration that this may be the representation of the Wheat and the thistles growing together within each one of us.

The Good News concerns what happens to us at the harvest. The harvest takes place at our physical death. At that point, God sends the harvesters to bundle up the sin that has been growing within us and casts them from us never to return. At the end of the parable the harvesters take the wheat placing it into the landowner's barn. In other words, the wheat that came from "pure seed" has now matured.

Once the harvest is complete you no longer hear about the field in the parable because after our physical death the human body or the field is no longer needed. The thought that you and I are the LOVE of Mother/Father God, made in the image and likeness of our heavenly Source in Christ Jesus, is quite liberating. If that is what the kingdom of God is like, then the anticipation of that day will certainly bring hope for all.

The Embrace

The thought occurred to me the other day about beginnings and endings. There are several ways to express such a thought. We could say "start to finish" or "A" to "Z". This kind of thinking is what has been described as linear. Linear thinking may be described by drawing a straight line with a pencil. Where the start of the line began would be the beginning and where the line stopped would be the end. I don't mean to insult the reader's intelligence, but what I would like to raise up for consideration tends to stray away from linear thinking.

It is recorded that Jesus seemed to make similar remarks that could be understood on a linear basis. He claimed to be the alpha and the omega, the beginning, and the end. There is a belief that the world began with creation and due to all the corruption one day the world will come to an end. I don't believe that, although I was raised to believe such. What I would like to suggest is an abandonment of linear thinking with the idea of embracing spherical thought.

What I am suggesting relates to the idea that our Heavenly Mother/Father God is an ageless being or Light. Because our Heavenly Source is ageless, all of creation is also ageless. So here is what I am suggesting. Take the pencil with which you drew the straight line and instead draw a circle. Take the first letter of the English alphabet "A" and place it on any point of that circle. Now take your pencil and follow the line around the circle until you come to the letter "A" once again. Beside the letter "A" place the letter "Z." What you have a picture of is the ageless nature of our Heavenly Source. There is no beginning or end but what I desire to draw your attention to, is related to what is inside the circle.

What is inside the circle is what our Heavenly Mother/ Father God embraces. What does Love embrace? You and Me. We are inside the embrace of our Heavenly Source and when Jesus came to earth, he came to "show us the Light" The way Jesus showed us the Light was by mirroring our Source's love. There is no end to Divine love. Because Jesus was and is the visible representation of the invisible God, Jesus claimed to only do what he saw the Divine doing. All the miracles Jesus performed were being performed by our Heavenly Mother/Father God. We too, are visible representations of the invisible God.

One other thought regarding the ageless nature of our Heavenly Source pertains to the distance between the east and the west. Jesus said, "As far as the east is from the west, so far have I removed your transgressions from you. If you think about it, our transgressions continue the journey away from us as far as the east is from the west. So, the next time you give consideration to beginnings and endings, please remember the ageless nature and embrace of our Mother/ Father God that is not linear but spherical and in that understanding Love Has No End!

The Ego

This reflection is taken from a new understanding of the Ego acquired from A Course in Miracles (ACIM). As I continue to explore this ACIM journey, it is becoming apparent that the ego only serves itself. In other words, it will offer only the thoughts that project fear and mis-trust when we encounter Truth. I have dealt with fear most of my life and I did not know why fear was so prominent until I began to investigate its origin. Once again, in ACIM, the major statement of understanding says, "Nothing real can be threatened, nothing unreal exists, herein lies the peace of God."

Following this line of thinking would suggest that the ego is not real and fear or anything that causes one to feel threatened or made to feel less than, does not exist. But that does not mean we cannot embrace fear. If we choose to embrace fear, then fear becomes quite real to us. Such thoughts bring to mind certain bible passages that have given pause to rethink what was being communicated. For example, in the Amplified Bible, in II Timothy 1:7 it plainly states, "For God has not given us a spirit of fawning fear, but of power, love, and of a well-balanced mind." If ego only serves itself, then it occurs that self-serving attitudes project falsehood's meaning that the ego can lie to protect itself. If the ego lies to protect itself, then what was being shared by Jesus in the gospel of John chapter eight and verse forty-four, as he spoke to the religious Pharisees, may indicate an understanding when one fails to see Truth. He even tells them that their search of scripture to find life is to no avail while Life was standing right in front of them being Jesus sharing the Christ energy that they did not recognize.

As I continue this journey, it occurs to me that if "satan" was a liar from the beginning, and I am of the opinion that "satan" is an entity or a way of thinking, then perhaps the ego was being highlighted because of our determination to run from those things that are threatening and cause fear. We are tested by fear. We would not know what fear is unless we experienced it. The Truth of love is what sets us free! Jesus made it abundantly clear that "You shall know the Truth and the Truth shall make you free, and if Jesus, (who came to teach the Christ energy), shall make you free, you shall be free indeed."

I continue to listen to the near-death testimonies of those you have had such experiences and they are helping me to better understand that we all are eternal, ageless beings. We came to this planet to experience a sense of separation that we did not know on the other side of the veil. Once we begin the awaken to our true reality of who we are and where we came from, we begin to abandon the lies told to us by the ego. This will bring about the reality of our true selves which is love and then we will begin to treat others by reflecting the love to all those we encounter. In doing so, we increase the spiritual vibration within ourselves which is best described as LIGHT!

The Cost of Distractions

I looked up the definition of "parable" and what I read was that a parable was a short allegorical story designed to illustrate or teach some truth, theological principle, or moral lesson. The definition went on to indicate that a parable was a statement or comment that conveys a meaning indirectly by their use of comparisons, or an analogy. I would like to hold up the parable located in the gospel of Matthew chapter twenty. It is the parable of the "laborers in the vineyard."

As the story goes, Jesus is telling the listeners what the reign of the heavens is like. He tells them that a householder went forth one morning to hire workmen for his vineyard. The workmen he hires all agree to be paid one denarii. So off they go to begin their work in his vineyard. The householder goes back to the marketplace about nine o'clock that morning and finds others idly standing around and he hires them. He tells them when it is time to receive your wages, whatever is righteous I will give you.

The householder goes back to the marketplace again at noon and at three o'clock in the afternoon hiring additional workers for his vineyard telling them as well that at the end of the day whatever is righteous, I will give to you. Now quitting time was at six o'clock in the afternoon but the householder goes back to the marketplace one more time at five o'clock, one hour before quitting time, and invites additional laborers to work in his vineyard. When six o'clock arrives, the householder calls his steward to gather the workers together and pay them starting from the last to enter the vineyard to the first.

When the last hired are paid, they receive one denarii. When the workers that had been hired at six o'clock in the morning discovered that those that had only worked for one hour got paid the same amount they were going to be paid, they began to voice their disapproval thinking because they had worked all day and in the heat that somehow they would receive more than the one denarii they agreed on before they began their work. The householder reminds the workers hired at six o'clock in the morning of their agreement to work for one denarii. So, he tells them that he is not being unfair and that they should take their wage payment and go their way.

The householder indicates that he is not doing anything unrighteous by paying them what they all agreed to receive. After all, he said, is it not lawful for me to do with mine what I will? For sure, this is a most interesting parable. Since Jesus is telling us what the kingdom or reign of the heavens is like, it is not plain to the casual listener. I would, however, like to offer some thoughts that surfaced recently regarding this parable in one of my early morning meditations.

In my meditation the workers who had been hired at 6 am did not realize that the denarii they were receiving was Life that is present in the kingdom of God. The vineyard was in essence God's creation and the householder is God. Receiving Life and entering the kingdom occurs when one awakens and puts aside the ignorance of who they really are in Christ Jesus. Those hired at 6 am became distracted by those who entered the vineyard late in the day while receiving the same Life the early hirelings received. Can you imagine thinking that those who only remained in the vineyard a short time but were included and welcomed into the Kingdom of God would be considered by those who had labored in the vineyard all or most of their life to be less than?

What became overwhelming clear to me was what the early hirelings missed in their distraction. The vineyard is God's creation. We all are laborers together no matter when we began the laboring or for how long we labored. At the end of the day, they all received a denarii which represents Life and Oneness with God. To lose sight of Life and Oneness with God by thinking you should receive more because you have some sense of entitlement is a huge distraction!

I have been blessed to enter the vineyard. The longer I have been there, it seems, the more I am discovering the multiple layers of Life and Oneness with God. The paradox is certainly present. One may think that extended laboring would only be exhausting and monotonous. However, I am discovering joyful surprises in this vineyard. Because of the length of time spent there and the amazing fellow laborers I am privileged to work alongside, I am finding opportunities to learn from them and to share my joyful surprises with them and others. We are all laborers together even if one only labors for an hour. I have been privileged to witness these very special one-hour laborers in the children's hospital where I labored for five years. Even though they only remained for an hour, they made such an impression.

Be aware of distractions!

The Cemetery

I used to live in a neighborhood located across the street from a cemetery. The highway separating my neighborhood from the cemetery was a four-lane road complete with a turn lane in the center. Usually, traffic flowed with a fair amount of ease both north and southbound along this thorough fare. I recall when it was a two-lane road. One could almost hear the numerous sighs of relief once this country road was expanded to accommodate all the vehicles that utilized it due to the population growth of the area.

The cemetery looked like most I'd seen. The grounds keeper took very good care to cut the grass and trim the bushes. I remember attending a couple of graveside services there for friends that had died. I also recall a group of people lining the various paths that wind through the cemetery with luminaries so people could drive their cars through the cemetery at night during the Easter season to reflect on the death of Jesus.

One weekday morning I was late leaving home to get to work. As I approached the highway that passes between my neighborhood and the cemetery, I noticed that the southbound side was backed up past the entrance to my neighborhood and it did not appear as though the traffic was moving at all. There is a two-lane road just on the other side of the cemetery. I noticed an occasional automobile traveling along that two lane road. Suddenly, the Bible passage in Matthew chapter seven came rushing into my mind, you know, the one that speaks about the difference between the broad way and the narrow way.

The broad way is said to be the path that leads to destruction and because it is so accessible many enter that way. The narrow way, on the other hand, leads to life and because it is so narrow few find its path. As I observed the numerous cars backed up on the four lanes highway, I began to consider the difference between the two roadways that were set before me. I could fall in line with the other drivers on the major highway and wait for the traffic to clear or I could make my way to the two-lane road. The only way that I was going to get to the two-lane road was to pass through the cemetery.

As I made my way through the cemetery suddenly the reality of that scripture began to explode within me. It was as though a light came on in my understanding. The only way one will discover the narrow way is to leave the broad way behind. The only way to leave the broad way behind is to awaken to life that is already within you. The cemetery represented my awareness that a death needed to occur to bring about life.

I have traveled that major highway lots of times but I shall never forget what was shown to me that morning as I made my way through the cemetery to reach a new understanding and awareness of the narrow road and the cost to get there.

The Builder's Heart

I grew up hearing people attempt to describe their observations of the Holy Spirit's movements by saying, "The Lord moves in mysterious ways, his wonders to perform." Later in life I heard another quote like the first one but with a more comical message, "The Lord moves in mischievous ways, our blunders to reform." At any rate, sometimes things occur that are difficult to explain. Often, because we can't explain them, we simply dismiss it from our thoughts like it never happened.

Today's reflection centers around extraordinary happenings that are often overlooked. Back in the late 1980s I was involved in chaplaincy training. This chaplaincy thing was very new to me. I began experiencing happenings for which I felt unprepared. I stood by bedsides of people who were suffering with all kinds of illnesses. Most of these hospital patients got well and were discharged home. Some of them, however, did not leave the hospital but experienced death.

I became well acquainted with numerous patients who were nearing death. I began to develop friendships with these special ones. I knew it would not be long before they would be taking their exit. One patient, for whom I had ministered, died in the night. I was not at the hospital when he took his flight. Upon my return the next morning, the deceased patient's family requested that I preach their husband, father's and grandfather's funeral. Up until that point, I had never preached a funeral. I had no idea how to go about preparing for a funeral service.

I sought advice from seasoned ministers as to how I was to prepare for my first funeral service. The directions I received were very helpful. I had served numerous congregations as their music minister before entering chaplaincy training. One pastor I had served with, right out of seminary, introduced a poem in one of his Sunday sermons. It was entitled, The Bridge Builder. This poem was created and written by Will Allen Dromgoole in the late 1800's. What is printed here is not how Will's poem was originally written, but rather how I first heard it spoken by the pastor I mentioned earlier.

An old man going on a weary way, came at the evening cold and gray
To a chasm vast and deep and wide through which there was flowing a swollen tide.
The old man crossed in the twilight dim, for the swollen stream held no fear for him,
And turned when on the other side and built a bridge to span the tide.
Said a fellow pilgrim near, "you're wasting your time with building here,
Your journey will end at the close of day, and you never again shall pass this way."
The builder lifted his old gray head, "Good friend in the way I've come," he said,
"There follows after me a fair-haired youth, and the swollen stream which held no fear for me, for the fair-haired youth may a pit-fall be."

While I prepared my first funeral service, I chose to finish my sermon with this Bridge Builder poem. I remember distinctly the family seated in the chapel of the funeral home. As I began to quote this poem the expressions on the faces of the family members began to show excitement. I recall the granddaughter let out a soft squeal as she motioned to the rest of the family. When I completed my sermon and offered a prayer of benediction, the family members indicated to me that this poem was a favorite of the deceased.

Additional conversations with this family aided me in discovering that this deceased patient had been a spiritual bridge builder for his grandson and the poem being utilized in his funeral service was not only his favorite, but it also emphasized how much of a blessing he had been to all his grandchildren. How was I to know this poem, that I first heard several years earlier, would be just what the family needed to hear as they remembered their loved one? The only explanation I can offer you pertains to the miraculous movements of the Divine Feminine Holy Spirit. Perhaps spiritual bridge building will assist each of us to encounter the miraculous while providing tangible relationships for those who follow in our footsteps.

Many years have gone by since my first funeral service was planned and executed. Since then, the Bridge Builder Poem has continued to speak truth about our need to help one another. That said, recently I have written additional verses to this poem to give awareness to the original message and the blessings given by the bridgebuilder. I have entitled it,

The Builder's Heart

*So, the builder finished the task at hand to help the youth better understand
When crossing a bridge, you did not build, the care of others to instill*

*For the fair-haired youth it did indeed increase awareness of the other's need
With careful thought to do the same in building bridges to heal the lame*

*So as the time has passed away the youth's fair hair has turned to grey
For others follow the builder's trail to discover a passage through the veil*

*And before that passage has come to pass doing for others will complete the task
For youth to awaken to the bridge's part is to discover the love in the builder's heart.*

Showing Up

I was introduced to music and singing in a choir while I was in elementary school. Of course, at the time, I had no idea music would play such an important role in my life. I received initial training to sight read musical notation while in junior high school. Tried out for a select ensemble in high school and was blessed to be chosen. Graduated from high school and entered college as a music major. How in the world I managed to make it through college and seminary while studying music remains somewhat of a mystery to me. However, if I had not shown up to participate in the first place, I would have missed out on so many blessings.

Serving as a minister of music in several churches in the southeastern United States helped me begin to grasp some of the challenges that often surfaces while being involved in "church work." Some of my experiences were very uplifting and some were, well, not so much. What I discovered about myself, during these challenging experiences, amounted to my lack of self-awareness. Now self-awareness is a fancy term describing how one becomes attuned to not only what they are doing but why they are doing it. Do you recall reading the passage in the Bible where Jesus looks out at the crowd while he is hanging on the cross and prays to his father in heaven saying, "Father forgive them for they know not what they do"? Perhaps it is important to know why we do what we do. Perhaps not knowing is why history repeats itself. At any rate, for a long time, as I think about it, I really couldn't tell you why I did what I did. I recall being challenged, by one of my supervisors, to find out. This happened while I trained to be a chaplain. That started my quest to make such a discovery.

I was asked why I wanted to train to be a chaplain. I really didn't know. My supervisor told me to go find out. I suppose I could have looked in several places to make such a discovery, but I chose to look in the Bible. I referenced an Amplified Bible and while reading II Corinthians 7:5-6, I made a most unique discovery. In Paul's letter to the Corinthians, he recounted the struggles he encountered while introducing the Gospel to the gentiles in Macedonia. Amid his pain and depression, he describes experiencing comfort at the arrival of Titus. Titus was perhaps Paul's first gentile convert. When Titus showed up, he brought with him a sense of encouragement that perhaps he did not even realize he possessed.

Suddenly, I became acquainted with my reason for being a chaplain. I don't often know the needs of people to whom I minister but somehow showing up brings a sense of comfort and encouragement that may be just what is needed.

Another thought regarding the existing presence of each of us may mean that we are already present with those needing our support. If that is true, then how we think and what our thoughts create for those in need opens doors for the vibration of love to bring the healing that needs to be shared. Often, we are not even aware of the blessings our presence brings to those who are in need. It is all based on love and when our attitude is loving and compassionate, the feminine energy that exists within each of us is projected out into the universe and that energy accomplishes untold healing even though we are not aware that this healing power is caring for the other.

Showing up is the most essential aspect of relationship. Showing up is necessary if one plans to participate. As I face each new year, I'm asking myself, "how will you show up for others? I think it's a good question to ask! I encourage you to ask it too. By so doing, hopefully we will be showing up for those who need us the most!

 Recognition

Have you ever considered the term recognition? To be positively recognized for some good deed particularly in the public eye brings with it a sense of wellbeing. To recognize someone for something negative however is mostly accompanied with regret and often with shame. This reflection speaks of how recognition has the power to open the door of understanding in a way that can be life changing. Here are three instances concerning recognition in hopes that a light will shine on that open door.

The conversation between Nicodemus and Jesus of Nazareth, as recorded in John chapter three of the bible, offers a recognition that we as humans need to recognize. Once Nicodemus tells Jesus that he and all his pharisee companions know that Jesus came from God because he could not do the signs he did unless God was with him, brings about a most remarkable response from Jesus. He says to Nicodemus that he could not "recognize" anything that came from God's domain unless he, Nicodemus, came from that domain to begin with. Of course, Nicodemus did not understand Jesus' response but as time went along the relationship that developed as a result of becoming aware of such a recognition that we all come from God's domain, literally changed his life.

The next recognition story is recorded in II Kings chapter six of the Old Testament. The story is about the siege of the walled city of Dothan where the prophet Elisha and his servant were at the time. The siege was taking place because the king of Syria believed Elisha was a spy for Israel. The king believed this because Elisha was hearing from God and taking what he heard to the Israelite army that kept them from being ambushed. The king sent a rather sizable army to surround the walled city just to capture one man, Elisha. When Elisha's servant arose from his sleep from the night before, he discovered this vast army encamped around the city. He goes an awakens his master asking what they were going to do. Elisha tells his servant not to worry because they that be with us are more than they that be with them. Elisha's servant was not sure just what he meant until Elisha prays asking God to open the eyes of his servant so he could see what Elisha was already seeing.

When the servant's eyes were opened, he "recognized" the mountains around the walled city to be full of horses and chariots of fire. This recognition by Elisha's servant suddenly brought about a new understanding resulting in putting aside his fear while trusting in the power of Mother/Father God that he did not see until his spiritual eyes were opened.

The last example comes from the New Testament of the bible in the book of Galatians and the first chapter. As the apostle Paul is writing this letter, he defines the message he is proclaiming based upon a spiritual recognition. He writes that it pleased God to separate him from his mother's womb revealing the Christ energy in him. When we "recognize" that this Christ energy is already within us and the Divine presence within us is not of our doing, this recognition has the power to literally and spiritually change our lives from the inside out.

There is much encouragement for those of you who find yourselves right here, right now, to consider how such a recognition that is awaiting discovery within you will ignite you by simply acknowledging it. In doing so, you will proceed through that open door of understanding into unlimited spiritual freedom. I dare you to take that next step!

Paradox

This reflection centers around the idea of paradox. Perhaps it would be helpful to take a moment to explore the various ideas that tend to support paradox and its meaning. Wikipedia defines paradox as, "a statement that, despite apparently sound reasoning from true premises, leads to a self-contradictory or a logically unacceptable conclusion. "A paradox is a statement or concept that contains conflicting ideas.

As I have considered paradox and how this idea has begun to take shape in my thinking, the more it seems to become increasingly shapeless. This shapeless form tends to speak in silence, move in stillness and exist in nothingness. I invite you to "enter" my reflection by "exiting" your possible pre-conceived ideas related to certainty. Remember, this is only a reflection. A reflection is the throwing back by a body or surface of light, heat, or sound without absorbing it." Therefore, perhaps to reflect reflections we will need to absorb what we will reflect.

I have discovered that my reactions tend to surface within myself as I use my senses to make judgements based upon that which I have determined to be reality. Whatever reality I have determined within myself to be certain it is from that vantage point where comes my judgements. Most of the time my judgements about others, for example, tend to come from what I see with my eyes or hear with my ears or experience with the other senses I have at my disposal. What if that which I deem to be certain begins to change and what I was so certain of no longer holds the weight it once did? What does that say about certainty?

It occurs to me that paradox may speak of passageways through opening that to the senses do not exist. Now if I were reading this for the first time, I might be thinking that the writer of this reflection is talking out of both sides of his mouth and there was a time when I would have agreed. But as I have explored some of the sayings of Christ, it is becoming clearer to me that paradox may have aided Jesus in putting the invisible right before our eyes inviting us to look at it with a different sense that perhaps we didn't know we had nor the ability to use.

In the gospel of Matthew of the Amplified Bible chapter 16 and verse 25, Jesus is recorded as saying, "For whoever is bent on saving his life shall lose it: and whoever will lose his life for my sake shall find it." Luke's gospel chapter 14 and verse 11 says, "For everyone who exalts himself (or herself) will be humbled, and he who humbles himself (or herself) will be exalted." Now these are just a couple of examples of the paradoxical nature of some of the sayings of Jesus. One of my favorite Bible stories that speaks to the paradoxical awareness of contradictory understanding appears in John's gospel chapter nine. This is the story about the man born blind. The blind man was treated by the religious establishment as a sinner due to his blindness. Therefore, to them he was a social outcast. Once he is healed of his blindness, he is given a new perspective regarding the outcasts of his day of which he is most aware. When Jesus finds him and asks him if he believes in the Son of Man, the outcast former blind man asks Jesus who he is so he can believe. Once Jesus identifies himself as being the Son of Man, the former blind man has absolutely no difficulty in believing Jesus to be the Son of Man. In other words, this young man who had been blind all his life was able to see Jesus for who he really is, the Son of Man.

The paradoxical idea of blindness becomes increasingly apparent when Jesus speaks of blind guides. He said they strain at a gnat and swallow a camel. He asks if the blind can lead the blind? Shall they both fall into the ditch? As I have continued to reflect on my own blindness, I keep on hearing the recorded words of blind Bartimaeus in Mark's gospel chapter 10. When I saw my blindness for the first time I cried out, "Jesus, thou Son of David have mercy on me" just like Bartimaeus did. Paradoxically speaking, for me to see, really see, I had to admit my blindness. When the Pharisee asked Jesus recorded in John nine if he were blind also, Jesus replied, "If only you had recognized your blindness, you would have no sin." That makes sense since Jesus came to take away the sin of the world.

No. 23

Probably one of the most familiar psalms in scripture is Psalm 23. You know, the one that begins with the words, "The Lord is my shepherd." I've asked myself often why this psalm has such an amazing following. I confess that I too have found much comfort in the words of this psalm, but beyond that as I look at each phrase within this passage it occurs to me that there must be quite a bit of identification with the poet that penned these words. Perhaps the poet that penned these words knew something about suffering. Perhaps the poet, like each of us, looks for comfort because in our everyday lives we experience things we can't explain, and we need something to hold on to that will accompany us through the pains life often brings across our path. Walk with me as we look yet again at the message penned by the psalmist.

As expressed in the Amplified Bible, "The Lord is my shepherd." In this one phrase we find acceptance and inclusion. Have you ever been in a place where you didn't feel included? The idea that the Lord is "MY" shepherd gives those hearing the message that they have a place to be, a place to exist. It speaks of being a part of something much greater than us. It portrays the idea of connectedness. When Jesus told his disciples that He had other sheep that were not of this fold that he needed to include as well certainly spoke of a fold much larger than the one his disciples imagined that included Jews and Gentiles alike.

As the psalm continues, "... I shall not lack," may indicate that because the Lord is my shepherd, he supplies just what I need. This idea of having our needs supplied may just be what people hold on to when they struggle with their surrounding circumstances. The Apostle Paul indicated that God would supply all our needs according to His riches in glory in Christ Jesus.

"He makes me lie down in green pastures." If you have ever had the privilege of watching a shepherd tend his or her flock of sheep it does not take long before you begin to understand that the shepherd's ability to lead their sheep to the best grazing land becomes quite a benefit for their flock. The healthier the sheep continue to be the more they will produce and reproduce. It has been said that only when a sheep feels safe will it lie down.

The shepherd leads his or her flock to the safest places. The scriptures indicate Jesus saying, "My sheep hear my voice and I know them, and they follow me." For those hearing the words of the poet we quickly insert ourselves into that green pasture where we experience the trust and love of the shepherd and the magnificence of our surroundings.

"He leads me besides the still waters." As I pondered this phrase, I recalled reading something that assisted me in the following thought. Still waters unlike rushing waters will allow us to see our reflection. Is it possible that it is beside the waters of reflection that we remember who we are, that perhaps much like the prodigal son, we need to experience that moment of coming to ourselves to remember who we are and whose we are? It occurs to me that the Good Shepherd would lead us by such a place so we can see ourselves as the Shepherd has always seen us.

"He restores my soul." As I have pondered this phrase, it is beginning to make sense to me that the restoration of soul is what naturally occurs when we discover ourselves in the Good Shepherd's flock, grazing in green pastures and awakening to our true reflection and seeing ourselves as Mother/Father God sees us. As we experience that warm embrace and know that our inclusion within this sheep fold was of God's doing and not ours, we begin to see ourselves as the restored people that we are in the Christ Energy. It is also necessary to understand when we come to school room earth, we come to learn how to love one another that increases our spiritual vibration. Once we come here, our higher soul remains in paradise that Jesus spoke of to the thief on the cross. Once we complete our earthly journey, we once again are restored to our higher self or soul thus the words, "He restores my soul or life."

"He leads me in paths of righteousness." God is a righteous God and because God is righteous, we follow God's righteousness. Unfortunately, there are times when perhaps due to circumstances, one may choose to go astray. However, the hope in this sheep going astray is that the Good Shepherd will leave the rest of the sheep in safety within the fold and will embark upon a journey to continue looking for this one who has gone astray until he finds it. The amazing thing about this picture of being lost is that this sheep cannot be lost unless it belongs. And the shepherd does all of this for his name sake because we all bear God's Name. We belong to the Shepherd!

"Even though I walk through the valley of the shadow of death I will fear no evil." I suppose we all have a working definition of "evil." As I have pondered my own definition of evil, I am becoming aware that evil is what occurs when I lose sight of my identity in the Christ energy, and I forget who I am and whose I am. When I do this, then I no longer see myself as the Good Shepherd sees me. Unbeknownst to me I begin reflecting an attitude of fear and death. If I retain my focus of my inclusion within the fold of the Good Shepherd being aware that I'm there because God placed me there, then walking through the valley of the shadow of death becomes much easier because I know that I am not alone for the Shepherd is with me. The Shepherd's rod and staff bring much comfort to me. As a matter of fact, this comfort is emphasized within me when I experience the Spiritual anointing presence which overflows my life.

"Surely goodness, mercy and unfailing love shall follow me all the days of my life and through the length of days the house of the Lord shall be my dwelling place." What a fitting end to this marvelous psalm. The promise that the fold of the Good Shepherd will continue beyond this life is perhaps the most dramatic and comforting words we can hear. These words take us beyond the unknown. It occurs to me that every blessing that is offered within this psalm will also continue beyond this life. The Lord is MY Shepherd and WE are the sheep of the Shepherd's pasture. So, enter through His gates with thanksgiving and into His courts with praise. Be thankful unto him and bless his Name for the Lord is Good and God's mercy is everlasting, and God's truth endures to all generations.

Moving Out

As a four-year-old child my family sought to teach me how to swing a baseball bat so I could hit the ball they would pitch to me. They soon discovered that my inability to hit the ball was connected to the fact that I couldn't see it. My father suggested that I turn around and swing left-handed and sure enough I hit the ball. To this day I continue to swing left-handed which only caused my family, at the age of four, to ask the question, "... what's wrong with Al's left eye?" That question was soon answered after an appointment to see the ophthalmologist. I was diagnosed with an eye condition called amblyopia better known as lazy eye.

Soon it was decided that I would enter the hospital to have surgery to correct my vision. After surgery and for the next ten years I experienced therapy related to strengthening the muscles associated with my left eye so it would work in tandem with my dominant right eye. I have worn glasses all my life and every time there was a prescription change in my lenses, I would have to get my eyes dilated. Nowadays it only takes eye drops for dilation to occur. Back in the late 1950s and early 60s it was accomplished with eye salve that once applied took two days to reach full dilation and two more days for the dilation to subside.

This condition affected everything. I had to do eye exercises while wearing a patch over my right eye. I absolutely hated these exercises. I had to wear this patch to school while I was in kindergarten and first grade. Of course, I had to sit on the front row so I could see the black board. My classmates made fun of me because of the patch I wore daily. Did I mention that I hated to read? My mother would order the "weekly reader" and make me read it. It was a condition I had to meet before I could go outside and play. Little by little my left eye began to improve and soon I had reached the point that I didn't need therapy anymore!

The surgery I had received at the tender age of four was explained to me like this, "... the muscles associated with your left eye were so strong that they were pulling your eyeball in toward the bridge of your nose. The surgeon clipped these muscles making them weaker so that the eyeball would eventually return to its center position so your vision would return to normal."

For a while that is what it did until sometime in the year 1986 at the age of thirty-three the sphere of the eyeball began to rotate further and further away from the bridge of my nose causing severe double vision. What I discovered about double vision was a total surprise. The more my left eye tracked further away from its normal position, the more my left eye's line of sight looked the opposite direction. My real challenge came while driving my car. It's strange having two images of the same car coming at you and just before the car passes you the images come together. I tried to train myself to only look at what my right eye saw, but the double vision was driving me insane.

I was serving a church in Augusta, Georgia at the time. There were issues that surfaced during my tenure there that was very disturbing. My feelings were hurt due to these issues as they affected my family as well. To say the least, I was holding quite a grudge toward those who I felt hurt my feelings. All of this occurred while trying to find some remedy for my double vision. I had visited an optometrist to hopefully discover what, if anything, could be done for my double-vision. He told me that my eyes were so bad that his machine couldn't even measure them. He suggested that I make an appointment to see an ophthalmologist. Upon that visit he informed me that my left eye was moving out, meaning that the eye was rotating away from the bridge of my nose.

I was devastated by such news about my eye, but I was equally devastated because of the issues associated at the church I was serving and the grudge I was holding only became bigger and more pronounced. I did not know what to do. As I look back on this experience, the amazement regarding the movement of the Divine Feminine-Holy Spirit was unmistakable. Not long after my doctor's appointment, I was home watching the 700 Club on television. I had never watched the program very much. To tell you the truth, I'm not sure why I was watching it at the time. At any rate, what I experienced during this broadcast has brought such a sense of clarity. Perhaps it will for you as well.

I recall the host of the 700 Club that particular day was an African American by the name of Ben Kenslow. As I joined the broadcast, he was talking about holding grudges. He indicated that to hold a grudge toward someone really didn't hurt them at all, but it really would hurt the one holding the grudge even to the point of destruction from within. I recall doing some soul searching and decided to release the grudge I was holding toward those who had hurt my family and my feelings. What happened next nearly blew me out of the water.

As I sat there listening to Kenslow having what he termed "a word of knowledge" meaning he would identify someone in the television audience regarding physical or spiritual malady and if they would claim their healing it would be done for them. This was not something that I was accustomed to let alone ever participating in. Then suddenly, I heard these words from Kenslow, "There's someone out there with lazy eye and if you will claim your healing it is yours." My skepticism kicked in saying to myself that surely there must be numerous people in a national broadcast that suffers from lazy eye. However, it did get my attention. I recall the host went on to other areas of need but just before he closed that segment he said the following, "Oh by the way, that person with lazy eye, your eyeball is moving out and if you will claim your healing it is yours!"

I did not claim the healing at that moment. I rather chose to sleep on it while giving thought to what I had experienced. On the way to the church office the next morning I made the decision to lay claim to the healing of my lazy eye. To make a long story short, my doctor paved the way for a new surgery that had just been developed and after that surgery I was cured. But the biggest healing that I witnessed throughout this experience was the "moving out" of the grudge I held and the freedom I have received by letting it go.

Love

What I hope to convey in this reflection is yet another attempt to describe the indescribable of which poems have been written and songs have been sung. The word in question is simply "love." The dictionary defines love as a profoundly tender, passionate affection for another person. It also indicates that it is a feeling of warm personal attachment or deep affection, as for a parent, child, or friend. However, based on some of my personal experiences as a chaplain serving in various medical centers and psychiatric hospitals, I hope to draw the reader's attention to perhaps consider how it is that we as humans seem to struggle with loving others and loving ourselves.

As a hospital chaplain, I have had the opportunity to hear stories from patients relating things they have never told anyone else. These remarkable human beings have discovered a safe place to recount experiences that often occurred beyond their physical existence. The first time I listened to a patient describe their near-death experience, I knew the ground upon which I stood was holy. After this account was told to me, the patient indicated that she had never told it to anyone. When I asked why, she told me she thought others would think she was crazy having lost her mind. I thanked her for placing her trust in me and that I would carry her story with utmost respect and care and that I believed her. The expression on her face communicated a sense of relief and love. What is love and where does it come from?

If you have had any contact with people of faith and their familiarity with scripture you may have heard the phrase, "God is love." What exactly does that phrase mean? As I have considered this and other questions related to love, allow me to share my thoughts related to such questions. First, God, or however one wants to describe this power that is far greater than myself and in my finite understanding, believes God to be the sum of all that is, whether visible or invisible. I believe God not only exists but contains all that exists. I believe God is Spirit ultimately expressing knowledge, understanding and wisdom within what I understand to be Love.

Borrowing the words of the Apostle Paul from I Corinthians chapter 13 in the Amplified Bible, also known as the love chapter, "Love endures long and is patient and kind; love never is envious nor boils over with jealousy; is not boastful or vainglorious, does not display itself haughtily.

It is not conceited—arrogant and inflated with pride; it is not rude (unmannerly), and does not act unbecomingly, Love [God's love in us] does not insist on its own rights or its own way, for it is not self-seeking; it is not touchy or fretful or resentful; it takes no account of the evil done to it—pays no attention to a suffered wrong. It does not rejoice at injustice and unrighteousness but rejoices when right and truth prevail. Love bears up under anything and everything that comes, is ever ready to believe the best of every person, its hopes are fadeless under all circumstances, and it endures everything [without weakening]. Love never fails." Please consider that what was described in the Love Chapter of I Corinthian 13, is an accurate description of the Divine Feminine aspect of Source. I also hold to the belief that each one of us are made in the image and likeness of this amazing Love.

Listening to near death experience testimonies, one expression consistently surfaces. What is described is their awareness and sense of being drawn toward an unconditional love energy. As I considered this expression, the question came to me as to how these travelers were able to identify this energy field as unconditional love? It didn't seem to matter where on planet earth they had lived, when they left their bodies, they were able to recognize and describe love's energy field as unconditional. We all recognize the familiar and recognizing unconditional love is where we came from. If it is true, that we all came from and are made from unconditional love, then such an understanding will figure into additional questions.

How in the world can Love beings made in the image and likeness of Love treat one another with such disdain? How is it that human beings often seek to lord over one another taking advantage through fear? How is it that we have the capacity to mistreat one another and when this behavior is not put in check, can ultimately rob the other of their physical life? How do we as humans create such implements of destruction for the sole purpose of threatening one another because we are so power hungry and afraid of somehow losing it? As I have considered these questions, I have come to one conclusion. We have forgotten who we really are and where we really came from. We have collectively lost sight of our Mother/Father God of Love and the unconditional love energy from which we were made. Our ignorance is our undoing.

Jesus came to this world to "show us the Light of Mother/Father God." We as humans projected our own wrath onto God claiming it was God's wrath toward us. We sought to control each other by insisting that this God of wrath was hell bent on destroying us if we didn't behave the way we were told we should. I am convinced that Love not only wins but has won! The realization of what was included in Jesus' finale saying from the cross has overwhelmed my thinking. To begin to grasp what is included in his saying, "It is finished" may offer the reader the hope that will guide us all to remember just who we are in Christ Jesus. If we utilize our five senses, sight, hearing, touch, smell, and taste to understand the Spirit, we will fall short every time. Reach out with your spirit of which you have the capacity to communicate with our Mother/Father God of Love. Rely on the Christ energy within you and in so doing you will reflect this amazing vibration.

Letting Go

It's not easy to let go, especially when one has worked their entire life to obtain the material possessions that they convinced themselves was necessary to be content. So, for those who are experiencing their latter days, the time will come when every possession obtained will of necessity remain on planet earth. Depending on how precious these processions are to the obtainer and how much value is placed in them will determine the difficulty of the transition at the time of physical death.

The world was here before we were born into it and will be here after we leave it. For those who have spent much of their lives collecting material wealth including the energy spent in guarding such possessions have bought into the deception that the world is all there is. When this deception has taken root within, it veils over the truth of who we really are and where we really came from.

There is much to consider at this point. So, what is it about these earthly possessions that so controls us to the extent that they possess our very being? These objects do not have a will of their own. Yet for those who have placed their energies in collecting and securing them have essentially become the object's servant. Please consider the position with which your riches have maneuvered you. It is recorded in the New Testament gospel of Mark chapter 8, "What shall it profit a man if he should gain the whole world and forfeit his life or what shall a man give in exchange for his life?"

Consider the wisdom from Iris Lohrengel's book Born from Above: What Jesus Really Said.

"We are so busy. There is so much to do, and since we are ignorant about who we really are and what the purpose of life is, we focus on all the material things that exist in the world, desiring to possess them and to add them to who we think we are. We keep our minds occupied with objects instead of focusing on and being preoccupied with our true spiritual self. This is what deceives us, that we attach so much importance to the things of the world. Riches do not have value in and of themselves. All is transitory; nothing exists to be ours forever. Everything, absolutely everything, has to be given up at the moment of death; the only thing that remains is our spiritual richness and the love that we cultivate in our hearts— to share it with all of God's creation."

For the sake of your wellbeing and the time of transition in which we all will participate, begin the journey now of letting go of earthly possessions. Try to learn a lesson from the rich young ruler recorded in Luke chapter eighteen. He followed all the religious rules but when it came down to his status as a wealthy young man, he could not bring himself to part with his possessions nor his wealthy status. Remember, it all stays right here! Letting go is not easy but it's not impossible! Making the discovery of who you really are in the Christ energy Jesus came to teach us becomes the initial step of freedom that has always existed in the truth. There was an expression often utilized in Alcoholics Anonymous meetings. Simply put, "Let Go and Let God!"

Kinsman Redeemer

While attending Bible College, one of the sayings that I heard my professors say was, "... Christ is in the Old Testament concealed and in the New Testament revealed." The more I reflect on these words the more I increasingly become aware that there are numerous instances where various characters and stories found in the Old Testament's thirty-nine books seem to point toward the reality of this saying.

One incident that may shed light on this idea was when the gospel writer known as Luke, penned the account of the two men that encountered a stranger while walking the seven miles from Jerusalem to Emmaus following the crucifixion of Jesus of Nazareth. The account is found in Luke 24:13-35. One part that is so interesting relates to how this stranger "opened the scriptures" (the Old Testament) to these two men beginning with Moses and all the Prophets, explaining to them what was said in all the Scriptures concerning himself and the funny thing is they didn't even recognize him until he did something very familiar in the breaking of the bread while having fellowship around the supper table and suddenly their eyes were opened.

Another incident occurred in Nazareth, the place where Jesus grew up. It occurred on a Sabbath day. While seated in the local synagogue he is handed the scroll of the Prophet Isaiah. He finds the place in this scroll and standing up he reads, "The Spirit of the Lord is upon Me because She has anointed Me to preach the good news to the poor; She has sent Me to announce release to the captives and recovery of sight to the blind, to send forth as delivered those who are oppressed to proclaim the acceptable year of the Lord." (The word "Spirit" in Hebrew is the word Ruach, pronounced rooakh. It means breath or wind. It is a feminine word and describes how Jesus was able to bring the Divine Feminine back into balance with the Divine Masculine. Jesus received a lot of push back from the masculine religious leaders that eventually caused them to crucify him.) He later tells those in the synagogue that this Scripture has been fulfilled in their hearing. Jesus is quoting from Isaiah chapter 61: 1-2. Of course, in Jesus' day there were no chapter and verse numbers but what Jesus is telling each of them is that He is the one to whom the Prophet Isaiah was writing.

This reflection is centered around the Old Testament book of Ruth and how the character Boaz becomes a type of savior for Naomi and her daughter-in-law Ruth. Naomi returns to Bethlehem from Moab with Ruth because both of their husbands have died. It is at the time of year when the barley grain is being harvested. Because Naomi and Ruth were both widows, they had no one to assist them as a husband would by caring for their needs. Eventually Boaz notices Ruth as she is gleaning in one of the fields and inquires as to who she is. Once he discovers that she is Naomi's daughter-in-law he begins to take some interest in her by placing her in protected places to glean after the harvesters giving strict orders to the young men working in the fields not to touch her.

When Ruth inquires about Boaz, Naomi is recorded in the second chapter of Ruth verse twenty recorded in the Amplified Bible these words, "And Naomi said to her daughter-in-law, Blessed be he of the Lord who has not ceased his kindness to the living and to the dead. And Naomi said to her, the man is a near relative of ours, one who has the right to redeem us." In the Jewish property and relational law, the kinsman redeemer was that person who had the right to redeem a relative who had gotten into trouble. Perhaps they had to sell all their property due to a debt they could not pay and if that didn't satisfy the debt, they may have had to sell themselves into slavery. The kinsman redeemer, because of his prior relationship with them, had the right to redeem that person and get them out of trouble.

What is being held up for you to consider is the kinsman redeemer does not become related to you when you accept the redemption he offers. The only reason he can redeem you is because he is already related to you. If Jesus, representing the Christ energy, is our kinsman redeemer, then his ability to be that redeemer is because he already has a relationship with us. The moment Naomi alerts Ruth that Boaz is their kinsman redeemer an awakening or an awareness occurs within her that she already belongs. When we discover that our relationship with Mother/Father God in Christ Jesus already exists and that relationship does not come by our doing, then we can rest in the knowledge that our redemption is secure within our kinsman redeemer Jesus the Christ and because of that redemption, our debt is paid!

Judgement

This reflection will be short and sweet but please consider the value that is being held up for the reader. Judgement is often the result of a decision made concerning most anything. When it comes to God, judgement has often been defined as a decision made by God that will ultimately separate us from God's presence because of a decision we made not to believe or some sin we committed that would eventually cast the non-believer away. The idea of judgement has somehow invaded mankind's thinking and the only way we were told we could escape God's judgement was to become a believer in Jesus.

This kind of thinking comes from religious ideation utilized to control others. It has often been written about the gospel story recorded in John chapter nine of the New Testament of the Bible concerning the man born blind. There is a particular statement recorded at the end of the chapter that this reflection holds up for consideration. This statement is attributed to Jesus. He makes a curious statement that He came here for judgement. Because of the mindset of mankind indicating we just don't measure up and we were born in sin, if we don't do what man says we must do in order to be accepted by God then God will banish us from God's presence.

What if the mission of Jesus was to come here to take away this mindset of separation from God once and for all? In Romans chapter eight it is written that "nothing" shall separate us from the love of God. In other words, "coming here for judgement," recorded in John chapter 9, is indicating that Jesus came here for our judgement that we applied to ourselves for the express purpose of taking it away. Judgement comes from the Greek word krisis which indicates separation. When Jesus was recorded to say, "Judge not lest you be judged," then considering the idea of separation as judgement, perhaps what Jesus was telling his hearers, and to us today, "don't consider yourselves separated from one another so you won't feel as though somehow you are being separated from God because of sin." Jesus continued his conversation in John nine by indicating that to recognize your blindness means that sin is no longer a mindset that separates you from God or one another.

Once you awaken to the love Mother/Father God has for you in Christ Jesus, and that this love is what motivated him to rescue us from our self-made judgement crisis of being separated from each other and God, then you will begin to reflect the heart of God and Love will cause your blindness to be recognized and the Truth will set you free!

Joy Comes in the Morning

As I continue my life's journey, I have bumped into all kinds of situations serving as a hospital chaplain. Some of these events are rather joyful. Some of them are downright painful. Some time ago I was called to come into the hospital's emergency room in the middle of the night to offer what comfort I could to a family whose child had a severe head injury. While the medical team worked to stabilize the infant, I stood outside the trauma room offering prayers for the child and his family. As the child began to stabilize, I received another page indicating an additional situation in the pediatric intensive care unit upstairs on the second floor. I arrived in the PICU and located the patient in question. The situation I discovered continues to surface in my memory years after its conclusion.

As I entered the pediatric intensive care unit it was obvious, due to the number of medical personnel present near the patient's room and the expressions on their faces that whatever was going on was serious and sad. Once I was briefed about the situation, I understood fully its seriousness. Seems this patient had been sick for quite some time. She was only two years old. She had been placed on life support weeks earlier in hopes that something medical could be done to reverse her painful dilemma.

One of the outstanding truths I have discovered about serving as a hospital chaplain remains for me somewhat bittersweet. I recall early in my career getting off the elevator on my way to see a patient one Saturday morning only to be met by the patient's young adult sister seated on the floor in the hallway. She was waiting for her parents to arrive at the hospital to visit their very sick teenage son. I had spent some time with the family days before but this Saturday morning the patient had taken a turn for the worse. When the patient's sister saw me coming down the hall toward her, she exclaimed emphatically, "Don't let my parents see you!" Often because chaplains are called to end of life situations, our presence seems to communicate a reality that some are not quite ready to grasp. This was the case then and I wondered what I was walking into that night in the PICU.

Different people see chaplains in different ways. Some see us as those offering comfort at the bedside. Others perhaps see us as representative of God.

Often when the patient is a helpless child and the prayer for that child seems to have fallen on deaf ears, the chaplain can feel the frustration and anger being expressed heavenward. As I stood silently just outside the patient's room, I simply observed the comings and goings of the various medical personnel and those who were there to support the patient's siblings. Soon I was invited to enter the room by the patient's mother. She asked me to please say a prayer for her daughter.

The decision had been made to disconnect the patient from life support because there was not anything else medically, they could do to save her life. I shall never forget the encounter I had with the patient's father. As I stood outside the room, he walked up to me and expressed his anger with God for not sparing his daughter's life. He indicated that this whole situation was not sitting with him very well. As I listened and felt his terrible pain I simply said, "I would be upset and angry too!" This was not the time to try to defend God as if I thought I could. God does not need our defense. God, I believe encourages us to be in the moment and listen for the pain and offer the ministry of presence.

What happen next, I was not anticipating. The father of the patient asked me if I would be present at the bedside when they removed the life support. This request may not seem like much but believe me it was monumental. Despite his anger with God he still wanted God's representative present as he held his daughter in his arms and said his goodbyes. The scripture says to be angry and sin not. If you don't think God can handle our anger, then perhaps your God is not very big. His love and compassion overwhelms our grief and our worst situations. My hope is there is a re-union coming where God will wipe away every tear. So, hold on my child. Joy comes in the morning!

Imagination

Let's say you imagined a world that existed within your imagination and whatever you decided you wanted to exist within that world was present. Let's say you decided to give your creation the ability to grow and develop on its own. As this growth and development takes shape, the freedom you have allowed has taken on a created life of its own with unexpected outcomes. Some of the outcomes are positive and some not so much.

Let's say the "not so much" positive outcomes are tending to overcome the positives. At the beginning of your venture with this created-imagined world, you were very pleased with what you had imagined. So rather than re-imagining this world you created, due to the negatives, you sought to influence your created world from within.

The world you had imagined had taken on a kind of darkness or confusion causing the creatures existing within it to begin behaving in a way not customary to your first thoughts of them. You were aware of how much you cared for these creatures within your imagined-created world and because you had decided to give them the freedom to choose, that freedom figured into your love for them. Because they now existed within this darkness, you devised a plan to bring them your light to overcome this darkness and help these creatures gain understanding.

Your plan was to imagine yourself as one of these creatures by going to where they existed within your mind to join them within the darkness with which they had imagined. Their imagination had veiled their original reality that you had imagined them to be in the first place. The darkness they were experiencing was so dark they were blind to the light you represented hindering their reflection of it.

You even sought to use your imagination to heal some of their issues hoping that would help them to see the light. Some of them saw it but those who did not thought you were a threat to them. Because all of this existed within your thoughts, each creative offspring coming into view was a testimony to your loving nature that each one was worth the journey. As time progressed, it became apparent to finally do away with the darkness, a new imagination had to be recognized that did not upset the freedom that already existed for the creatures you first imagined.

As the darkness continued to exist still feeling threatened by your light, eventually the darkness that controlled the creatures set into motion their own plan for snuffing out the light completely. Once the creatures had assumed they had extinguished the light and claiming victory for their darkened confusion, their very act set into motion your determined imagination that your light would be unveiled within every creature you had ever imagined freeing them from being controlled by their darkness. This freedom allowed each creature to remember how they were first imagined by you. Each creature exists within your thoughts and not one of them exists outside of your thoughts.

Surrounding your imagination is the spirit of your desire to create a world that reflects the love it took for you to create in the first place. It is that spirit that holds your imagination and seeks to awaken those who have yet to come to your light. It is just a matter of imagination before your created world is awakened from its slumber.

I invite the reader to use their imagination as you consider this reflection!

I can See

Some time ago while engaged in hospital chaplaincy ministry, I entered a hospital room to introduce myself to the patient. She was a warm and caring person and we seemed to hit it off right away. It was my custom to share my hospital business card with patients in case there was a need for them to get in touch with me later during their hospital stay. I placed the card on her tray table and continued to visit with her. I noticed that the patient's nursing light was on indicating that she had requested her nurse to come check on her. While I stood next to her bed chatting with her, the nurse knocked on the door to enquire as to what she needed.

It was a simple request. The patient indicated that because she could not see anything without her glasses and her purse was on a table across the room could she please retrieve her purse so she could put her glasses on. The nurse politely walked over to where the patient's purse was and brought it to her. She then asked if there was anything else she could do for her while she was there. The patient said she was fine for now so the nurse excused herself from the room.

As we continued our conversation it was certainly evident to me that this African American woman was very spiritually minded. Our conversation turned toward her deep concern for all the racial violence and bloodshed being reported in the news. I told her that I too shared her concern. Then I said to her, "A lot of people tend to look on the outward appearance but if they could see what we share within us, they would know that we are kin." The expression on her face at that moment was remarkable. It was one of those Holy moments that words just can't describe.

She asked me if I would pray for her. She requested that I pray for her home to be safe while she was in the hospital, and she also requested that I pray for the safety of her family too. We held hands as I voiced the prayer. Upon the conclusion of my prayer something happened that I can only describe as Divine.

The patient began to say over and over, "I can see! I can see! I can see!" With her hands raised she continued to express herself. I didn't exactly know what she was talking about, and I must have had a confused look on my face.

She reaches over and picked up the business card I had placed on her tray table, and she began to read aloud every word on the card. Then it became clear to me that she was reading my business card without her glasses.

As I have reflected upon this encounter, I am being made increasingly aware of the awesome presence of the Divine Feminine that is present within each of us. The healing power of the Divine Feminine surfaces through sound. When the Divine Masculine and Divine Feminine are balanced within us, then the miracles of healing, compassion and love are released into our present situation. As I continued to give this encounter additional thought, the message that I offered to this dear soul became healing that I was not aware was being projected out to her from the sound of my voice. The result of her now being able to see without the need for her glasses speaks to the healing energy we all have access to whether we know it or not.

Humility

Today's reflection centers around humility. Humility has often received bad press because it is sometimes confused with being fearful or perhaps showing signs of weakness. The Cambridge English Dictionary defines humility this way, "the feeling or attitude that you have no special importance that make you better than others; lack of pride."

When I consider humility, I often recount the biblical passage that deals with the paradoxical understanding of humility versus exaltation. This passage is in Matthew's gospel chapter 23 and verse 12. "And whosoever shall exalt himself or herself shall be abased; and he or she that shall humble himself or herself shall be exalted.

Let's pretend that you work in an office setting. Your supervisor is one that has little patience and demands strict adherence to office rules and regulations. On the surface this supervisor seems to have the company vision at heart but their attitude toward all of those working in the office alongside of you comes across as belittling and devaluing. As you attempt to adhere to your supervisor's demands you begin to sense perhaps a feeling of sadness or maybe fear that if you do not perform to your supervisor's expectations your employment will be short lived. When your boss is out of the office everyone seems to get along just fine but when they return that sadness seems to re-enter the office with them.

I can offer such a scenario because I have personally been there. On the surface I resisted the way the office staff, including myself, was treated. I confess a fair amount of resentment and hurt feelings. What I did not know I was receiving at the time became such an amazing gift that has served me throughout my career as an office administrator.

What we observe others doing, depending on our frame of reference, can either help or harm us moving forward. When I became a director of a pastoral care department in a hospital setting all my memories of being micromanaged came rushing back into that present moment. A decision was made that I was going to walk a different path. In other words, in that previous setting I was being taught how not to do things. At first this new path was very challenging particularly for those who had never had the opportunity to serve on a staff of a non-micro manager.

What I gained on this new path was an understanding of the effects of humility. Think about it. If I choose to lord my authority over you because of the position I hold, chances are you may resist that authority for a while. Should you buckle beneath that authority and remain present, it's just possible that the relationship between us will be fear based. On the other hand, should I approach you with humility seeking a genuine relationship, a new thought may register within you. You may ask, "can I trust this person or not?" Such a question is necessary for your observations to continue. If their humility is genuine then your estimation of that person grows remarkably.

Humility is also associated with giving. To give of yourself in love seeking to lift the other out of a pure heart will come back to bless you in ways not yet considered. Exaltation is not the reward for humility. If one truly humbles herself or himself, the reward will be the exaltation of the other. Once the understanding of giving is recognized, then the ability of receiving from Source will enable one to grasp the miracle that our loving Mother/Father God has given to all, and our receiving is necessary for others to receive as well. Remember, "God so loved the world that He gave…"

Green Light

Just the other day me and a couple of friends were looking for a restaurant in which to indulge our appetite. Because the friends who were with me were not from my state, I had driven them to the downtown area to allow them to take in the sights and sounds of our fair city. After they had taken all the pictures so to remember their sightseeing experience, we got back into the car to find that restaurant I mentioned earlier.

As we were proceeding to our destination, I noticed a car a couple of blocks ahead of me had turned on to the road I was driving on and it was going in my same direction. The driver of this car stopped at a red light and of course when I arrived at this intersection, I also stopped to wait for the light to change to green.

As we sat waiting for the traffic light to change to green, we continued our conversation related to the sightseeing encounters we had experienced during our weekend visit. Suddenly, the traffic light changed to green and the car in front of me didn't move. I thought to myself that perhaps the driver had not noticed the traffic light changing to green, so I waited. As I waited the thought occurred to me that perhaps the driver was looking at his cell phone and that was the reason, he remained motionless.

I have had experiences where I was the motorist first in line at a red light and because I was not paying attention when the light changed to green someone in the line behind me honked their horn to wake me from my distractions so all of us could proceed through the intersection. After waiting, for what seemed an unusually long time for this motorist to move forward I simply tapped my horn to hopefully draw his attention to the fact that the light was now green. What I received from this driver I was not expecting. While the driver continued to remain motionless, he raised both of his hands high enough for me to notice his crude and insulting gesture. In street speech the young man "flipped me off."

My first thought was, "you've got to be kidding!" After this young man's gesture, he then proceeded through the intersection and on to where ever he was going. At first it was difficult for me to make sense of this encounter. I was angry and at the same time hurt. I wondered if he had done all of this on purpose. At any rate I began to offer prayers for him and for myself. Then after giving this incident some time to simmer, I would like to share this reflection with you.

I've heard it said that the greatest desire Jesus has for us is to set us free. Being set free, it seems, only comes by knowing and understanding the truth. Jesus said he was and is the truth. I thought to myself, "how many people are sitting at spiritual green lights not knowing they are free to move forward?" How many people are imprisoned by their own distractions? They often fail to see the light they already have within themselves. And the most amazing thing that occurred to me came because of this young man's reactions. Whether he was aware of the green light or not when I tried to point him to the fact that he had the freedom to move forward all he could do was bring insult.

Loving those who bring insult is one of the hardest things we are called to do. It is easy to love those who love us. The prayer I pray for you and for myself is that I will take my freedom seriously to love those who for whatever reason have not yet awakened to the love and the "green light" they have inside their being. I believe that once they are shown the love of Christ they will be forever changed and forever free!

Fear

This reflection relates to the continuing journey away from what I was taught in the evangelical fundamentalist denomination of my childhood, adolescence, and young adulthood. The subject of this reflection is centered around "fear." When I heard the church leadership speak about "the fear of the Lord," and we needed to do that because that's what believers do to stay in God's good graces, what consistently came to my mind was "being frightened" of God because my childhood understanding was centered around the fear I had developed with my own dad due to the beatings I had endured from him. My dad had a certain facial expression that sent chills down my spine when I did something that did not please him and if a beating was the result of his displeasure in my behavior it only served as a transference in the identification of the wrath of God.

So, I decided to do a word study from the Ancient Hebrew Research Center (ancient-hebrew.org) What I hope to share with you relates to two Hebrew words translated "fear." The first word for fear is the Hebrew word "pahhad." The bible passage using this word is found in Job 4:14. *Fear (pahhad - noun) came upon me, and trembling, and caused all my bones to shake (pahhad - verb).* So pahhad as a noun, means "shaking" and the verb form is "to shake." The second Hebrew word for fear is *"yara."* There were two passages offered that used the same Hebrew word but had two different understandings of fear. Genesis 3:10 indicated fear from the standpoint of "being afraid" while Deuteronomy 6:13 gave an understanding of "yara" as "reverence." It was interesting to note that "yara" in its concrete literal meaning means, *"flowing of the gut."* Then the following question from this web-based word study site asked, "Have you ever been so scared or been in the presence of something so amazing that you could feel it in your gut?"

Suddenly, I began to piece together what happened to me that memorable Sunday morning back in 1976 in my college dorm room when I "Entered into His gates with thanksgiving and into His courts with praise" Psalm 100. The overwhelming sensation that I experienced occurred in my gut. It was a "flowing" experience that drew me in. I did not want this reverential fear to cease. What I am discovering is a whole new understanding of fear considering reverence. Reverential Fear does not expel you nor does it drive you away, rather it draws you in to safe places free of condemnation with an emphasis on praise.

The "fear of the Lord" based upon the theological information received from my childhood and young adult years was rife with misunderstanding. I was the one being accused of not pleasing the Lord. These accusations caused me to feel as though I was separated from God. That was a very fearful place. That is not to say that "fear" is not experienced. 2 Timothy 1:7 reads, "For God has not given us a spirit of fear, but of power and of love and of a sound mind. However, that does not mean we won't experience fear. It just means that when we do, KNOW where it is not coming from. Evil uses fear to control. Love does not control anyone or anything. Love casts out fear. Love embraces and through our ability to choose, we enter the kingdom of Mother/Father God because that is where we all come from. So put aside your fear and embrace a desire for the high vibration of the Light of God to enlighten you!

Face to Face

It is a mystery! It may be an assumption but there are a lot of people who enjoy a good mystery. You know, a kind of "who done it" where something has happened, and it is not clear where or from whom this happening occurred. In a world where there seems to be non-stop bad news, bearing the weight of responsibility to find the guilty party can be overwhelming and frustrating, not to mention disheartening.

But what if the mystery is centered around a happening that is absolutely wonderful? What if one day you and your community awaken to something that has been done for you that is so amazing and wonderful that it just left everyone speechless? What if everyone tries to discover the responsible party but no one steps up to take the credit? So, there you are basking in the pleasure of this wonderful happening with seemingly no one to thank.

This reflection has to do with awareness. Awareness is the key that unlocks mystery. Awareness can also be compared to an awakening. As I have journeyed along my path all my lack of understanding, particularly pertaining to spiritual matters, is best described as a mystery. Let me hasten to say that awareness is not something I generated or contrived.

When I first made the discovery that my existence did not begin on planet earth, I did not exactly know what to do with such awareness. When I discovered that my life is hidden with Christ in Mother/Father God, (Colossians 3:3) it was as though for a moment I got to peek behind the veil to view a reality so vast and overwhelming that all I could say was "wow!" When the gospel of John was penned, it did not begin as the other three gospels did. The gospel of John began with, "In the beginning was the Word and the Word was "with" God and the Word was God." I recognize the "Word" to be the Christ energy in Jesus of Nazareth. The word "with" is the Greek word *pros* meaning towards, face to face. In other words, to be face to face is to be intimately related. It is much like kissing. You cannot kiss or be kissed by your lover simultaneously unless you are face to face.

Then the discovery was made that yours and my beginning took place face to face with Mother/Father God. When we first became conscience of our spiritual reality we did so face to face with our Creator. Jeremiah 1:5 of the Amplified Bible reads, "Before I formed you in the womb I knew and approved of you." We exist because Mother/Father God loves and likes us. It is most interesting that while meditating on such mysteries the Divine Feminine Mother God, we often call the Holy Spirit, suddenly brought a familiar verse of scripture into my remembrance. The simplicity of it, considering this new awareness, is what was so overwhelming. In the Amplified Bible, I Corinthians 13:12 reads as follows, "For now we are looking in a mirror that gives only a dim reflection of reality as in a riddle, but then when perfection comes, we shall see in reality and face to face. Now I know in part; but then I shall know and understand fully and clearly, even in the same manner as I have been fully and clearly known and understood" Being "known" is what existence is all about. What is so wonderful about being known of Mother/Father God is that our Divine Light Source knows us all by name and we are known face to face.

Ears to Hear

In the five years ministering within a children's hospital, I have witnessed various things that have so overwhelmed me that I learned not to be surprised by anything. I am learning to take what I see in stride. When I consider what some of these precious children are having to deal with physically not to mention emotionally and mentally, I am simply amazed at these kids and their parents.

One day I noticed a little boy with his father. The little fellow couldn't have been more that four years old. Working in a children's hospital you hear children's voices a lot. Sometimes these voices are happy and playful and at other times they are expressing pain or sadness due to their present circumstances. This little guy was exercising his voice by sounding off at the top of his lungs.

Now ordinarily hearing a child's voice isn't anything to write home about. However, the situation I am describing here relates to why the little boy was making such noises. You see, this little guy had two cochlear implants on either side of his skull. He was so fascinated with his voice that he not only wanted to hear himself speak, he wanted everyone around him to hear his noises as well.

I walked up to him and his father, and I asked his father how long has he been able to hear his voice. The father said his son has been able to hear his own voice for about a year now. He told me that he does not wear the implants all the time but when he does, he just loves them and expresses himself like you are hearing him now all the time.

I was simply awed by this experience. I felt an emotional surge coming up from within me as tears began to flow from my eyes. Can you imagine what it must be like to not hear any sounds. From a child's perspective not hearing any sound would not mean much since the child would not have anything to compare it to. They would just go through their lives perhaps thinking what they are presently experiencing is normal. It would not be until someone who has hearing, like his or her parents, choosing to investigate the possibilities that their child is deaf, that something would be done about it.

This puts in place for me the idea of spiritual hearing. For those who are deaf spiritually, meaning they have not heard the sound of the Spirit of God that continually pours forth speech, tends to go through life in a kind of spiritual ignorance. Events happen whereby spiritual sounds go forth and there may be times when such sounds may be entertained but since they have nothing to compare this communication it just falls on deaf ears.

When those who have become familiar with the Spirit's communication lift the possibilities of hearing for those who have not, an awakening of sorts can happen opening up the presented possibility. Then the practice of the pre-existing ability to listen spiritually is invoked within the hearer and the continuation of their spiritual journey is confirmed. It is also understood that healing comes through sound and the sound of increasing spiritual vibration opens the portal for such healing to awaken within us.

Deja Vu

The concept of Deja vu has been defined as experiencing something or some place or someone that even though your physical senses are testifying to you that you have never been there or experiencing the moment yet there is a kind of familiarity with the moment that suggests that you are familiar with the moment you are experiencing. Please consider the following.

When Nicodemus comes to Jesus by night (St. John 3) he tells him with no uncertain terms that he knows Jesus comes from God because Nicodemus is convinced that Jesus could not do the things he was doing unless God was with him. To which Jesus tells him that he could not recognize that he, Jesus, came from God unless he, Nicodemus came from God to start with.

When humanity believed the lie that God was withholding divine likeness from us and the garden of Eden couple felt they needed to do something to be accepted by God, we sought to embrace that lie. We embraced it even though we were made in God's image and likeness to begin with. Once this lie was internalized, humanity began to walk down a path taking our God-given design, which was and is to reflect God's glory, and humanity began to reflect the lie to each other which amounts to darkness and fear and mistrust that leads to violence and murder.

Jesus Christ, the anointed one of Source, is our Deja vu. It is stated in the Old Testament book of Jeremiah 1:5 of the Amplified Bible the idea that our spiritual beings were known before our physical birth on planet earth. "Before I formed you in the womb, I knew and approved of you." I believe we knew God in the Christ energy before we were formed in our mother's womb, or we would not be able to recognize the familiar in Christ as did Nicodemus. In essence, we are not the physical body we occupy here on school room earth. We are Light beings incarnating to school room earth to experience the illusion of separation to remember who and whose we are. This kind of awareness is not available on the other side of the veil. This awareness is designed to increase our vibration so we can help others increase their vibration.

Jesus came to reflect the familiarity of Mother/Father God to us so the part of our being that already knew the Light would remember our true selves and embrace and reflect the Light once again for the Light has always embraced us! Once we catch a glimpse of this familiarity, that is absolutely at home within each of us, the sooner we will begin to recognize the Light in everyone we encounter. When that happens, the awareness of our true selves will be reflected for all to see. Then our amazing acts of kindness and compassion manifested by the Divine Feminine will assist those who have not discovered that they too are Light beings and will awaken to their true selves.

Condemnation

Have you ever been in a place where those around you, for whatever reason, made you feel less-than or condemned? It may have been something they said or perhaps a look they gave you that made you feel somewhat unimportant or rejected. It may have come from experiences from your past that reminded you of such a feeling. Whatever it was, if you are familiar with this "less-than" feeling that has communicated condemnation and that perhaps has an element of shame attached to it, then hopefully this reflection will offer the reader some words of encouragement.

There are plenty of words in the English language that are synonymous with feelings of condemnation. Here are but a few. Denounce, punish, belittle, adjudge, decry, criticize, disapprove, judge and damn. Often these depictions are projected from those who have experienced the same feelings and the way they have tried to combat it is to belittle others. Projecting on to others the pain we carry around with us, is a reminder of our human makeup that we are beings of reflection. When these painful feelings are projected, most of the time we are not even aware of what we project. Often, we seek to bury these painful experiences deep down within us thinking that if we no longer think about them then they must no longer be present within us. Please take a moment to reflect on the following statements. Painful experiences cannot be deleted from our history or our memory. The way they are encountered, moving forward, is when we are reminded of our painful situations by recognizing them in others. When that happens, we then become critical of the other not realizing that our critique of the other is based upon our own history of which we have tried to forget. It is the proverbial getting the spec out of your brother's eye when you have a log in your own eye.

If you have ever been bullied or been made to feel as though you are an outcast because of your social standing due to race or financial status, to name a couple, then you are not alone. Diversity, equity, and inclusion are terms that are very prevalent today and, in the opinion, shared here should be taken very seriously. Thinking about the ministry of Jesus, it is noted that he tended to side with the outcasts of his day. He ate with tax collectors and prostitutes and had his greatest conflict with the religious.

The religious of our day are everywhere. There seems to be as many opinions of religion as there are opinions. However, if Jesus fellowshipped with the tax collectors and the prostitutes of his day and related to the religious that these would enter the kingdom before them, then it is held up for your consideration that he also sides with those who have been or are presently being bullied and condemned.

Jesus came to this world to do away with condemnation. As it states in Romans chapter eight verse one of the Bible, "There is therefore NO condemnation to those who are IN Christ Jesus. So, the question being held up for us to consider, "are we in Christ Jesus? Is there something we must do to be in Christ Jesus? The evangelical world would probably say that there is something we must do. But consider this. If the salvation that God provides each of us in Christ Jesus had something that we had to do for this salvation to be officially ours, like accepting it, then would not it make sense that we would become the savior instead of Jesus? If we are saved by grace and that not of ourselves it's a gift of God, not of works, including acceptance, lest anyone should boast about it, (Eph 2:8 & 9) then waking up to what is already within us makes the gift of salvation possible because the Christ energy that Jesus revealed to be already within us means that what we came to school room earth to accomplish, is to remember who and whose we are. One cannot remember unless they were a member once.

When we discover this salvation is already apart of us, then that awareness has the power to change our entire being. We no longer must feel as though we must strive for something based upon our behavior like trying to please God to receive or better yet to maintain God's favor. When that becomes prevalent, then the condemnation we have experienced from others and from ourselves begins to wane away and we are free to reflect a "no condemnation" spirit to all those with whom we come in contact. Loving the other is not an easy task. But the more we reflect an unselfish love to and for others, the more they will begin to recognize the love of God that already exists within themselves as well.

Competition?

This reflection pertains to the subject and hopeful understanding of the term competition. After looking up the definition of *competition,* this is what was discovered:

The act of competing; rivalry for supremacy, a prize. A contest for some prize, or advantage: the rivalry offered by a competitor.

Humankind has been involved with competition seemingly forever. Competition has been observed in the workplace, the sports arena, religions, and belief systems and recently it has surfaced once again among various races of humans. I remember being told as a child, after joining a little league baseball team, "it's not if you win or lose, but how you play the game." At some point in becoming an adult, it was observed the complete turnaround of that statement. It was revealed that when a professional team, who had been successful with a winning record, no longer had such a winning record, suddenly, the head coach lost his head coach job. That does not seem to sit well with the saying I learned as a child. So, it appears that it really does matter if you win or lose.

What is it about us humans that entertain the thought that if we are not ranked among the successful in whatever arena we happen to be in that somehow, we just don't measure up? I know that a lot of what is driving such thoughts is our economy. We certainly want to be successful in what we contribute. However, if the definition is accurate that competition is rivalry for supremacy, once that supremacy has been secured, what happens to all those who did not obtain that supremacy? Whose voice stands out once the supremacy is reached?

This supremacy scenario is played out in the childhood game, "king of the mountain." Once the king position is reached by one of the children, then it becomes the desire of every other child to replace the king by knocking him or her off the mountain. Once an older and stronger child reaches that supreme position, the other smaller and weaker children typically have no chance to obtain that position. It is usually at this point that the game ceases to move forward because the king position will no longer be shared.

If that happens in our adult world and we feel as though that supreme position was obtained illegally or with unscrupulous intentions, then it is possible that the same unscrupulous kinds of means may be put into actions to rid the king of his or her position or the king may use unscrupulous means to maintain power.

Because this is a reflection, the sharing of these ideas with those reading this entry may introduce the struggles with the observations others have made over the years where the act of supremacy seems to have done more damage than it did to offer aid in each situation. It has been observed that people finding their way to the top, so to speak, may have changed their personality based upon what it took to arrive at the top. It was a reminder of Dr. Jekyll and Mr. Hyde. What occurred had to do with possible hidden agendas that only surfaced once the supreme position was obtained.

Please consider the scriptural concept regarding exaltation versus humility. If we exalt ourselves, we will be humbled. But if we humble ourselves, we will be exalted. The exaltation of being at the top must be promoted through humility. If one exalts himself or herself through selfishness, then that same selfishness will continue to drive that person's supremacy. However, if one reaches that position of supremacy because humility motivated them to love and care for the others around them, then there is no competition. I really don't believe competition is of Mother/Father God. Can you just imagine experiencing death and suddenly you find yourself in a new and different place and while encountering a being of light and the first question you pose is, "where do the kings of the mountain people hang out?

Born Again?

I read a quote the other day that said, *"Truth does not invite dispute, doctrine does!"* In my opinion this statement sums up most if not all the arguments I have heard and even participated in with those in evangelical circles as it relates to being "born again." When I began to grasp the truth that John chapter three, verse three of the Bible was incorrectly translated my whole theology began to take on a freedom that is easy to describe for those who have seen it and difficult for those still listening to the doctrine of "salvation" that spun from this misinterpretation.

As I have sought to relate this idea in other blog entries, I cannot overemphasize the depth of truth that I seek to share with the reader. Please allow me to explain. I believe it is safe to say that the cornerstone of Evangelical denominationalism is salvation. Salvation, according to the King James Version of scripture is related to being born again as is stated in John 3:3. This idea of being born again is often surfaced in conversations with over-zealous evangelicals seeking to get the potential "lost sinner" saved by asking the question, "...have you been born again?"

Of course, for the unsuspecting recipient often the answer to such a question is, "I don't know." This is music to the ears of the one sharing their understanding of salvation. Most of the time if not all the time the understanding of salvation that is being shared is just repeated words based upon their own so called salvation experience. There is even a "plan" of salvation that these evangelicals can walk one through so they can get their recipient to pray the "sinner's prayer" so they can invite Jesus Christ to come inside of them so they can go to heaven when they die.

I know this to be true because I was trained in religious colleges and seminaries how to do this so people would not die and go to hell. This is based upon the misconception that sin separates us from God and if we are labeled "sinners" then we are believed to be separated from God. So, to not remain in such a hopeless state, we are told that our main Christian purpose is to seek and to save those who are lost and bring them to salvation in Christ. That sounds pretty good on the surface. But for the countless numbers of people who continue to struggle with the notion of whether they did the steps of this so-called plan of salvation correctly, I write this reflection.

Discovering the truth that "NOTHING" can separate us from the love of God which is in Christ Jesus begins to chip away at the "doctrine" of salvation that has so mis-guided millions. Being born again is not what was being shared with Nicodemus as recorded in John 3:3. Jesus was telling him that his ability to recognize that He came from God based upon his observance of the miracles Jesus performed was proof that Nicodemus was "born from above as well otherwise he would not have come to such a conclusion. As a friend of mine put it, the misinterpretation "born again" was never used like that anywhere else in scripture. The Greek word "anothen" which means from above was interpreted "from above" in all its other instances.

So where does that leave us? To make this discovery may put one at odds with those who still hold to the notion that one must be "born again" to receive salvation. Think about it! To accept the idea that we were "born from above" to begin with, would mean that salvation is an awakening to what one already possesses which is essentially the meaning of grace. This possession in not of our doing nor of our creation. We were created IN the Christ energy that Jesus came to reveal. We have always been IN Christ Jesus and to awaken to this amazing fact is what frees us from "doctrines" that misguide and or misconstrue. All of that to say, this truth is not intended to be forced upon anyone. That is not my intention. What I would offer to those reading this reflection is simply to give what I have shared here some consideration. Once truth becomes visible, doctrines are visible no longer!

Being Spirit

Where did we come from? How did we get here? Who is responsible for our existence? These and other such questions have been asked repeatedly throughout the countless generations of human existence. Science has tried to give evidence to such questions. Theories have been placed into our thinking to give us answers. Yet generation after generation these and other questions continue to be posed. Because this is a reflection, I am simply offering something for the reader to consider. The answer to these and other questions may lie in our ability to see beyond our physical selves, perhaps peering into what has been termed spirit.

I often wonder if our physical existence can hinder our ability to see and experience our spiritual existence. Spirit has been described as "breath." In the Genesis account of creation God "breathes" into what he has formed from the dust of the ground and mankind became a living being. Jesus refers to the Spirit as "wind" in the gospel of John chapter three as he spoke to Nicodemus. Becoming aware of ourselves as "spirit" may open a whole new way of understanding.

In the bible account found in Jeremiah the first chapter and the fifth verse, he records a spiritual understanding that God knew him before he formed him in his mother's womb. As I have considered this thought, I have often asked myself, "where did you know me?" You know how it is, one thought cascades into other thoughts and before you know it you are lost in an overwhelming array of more questions. But what if our existence before we were born here on earth was in a spiritual state. A spiritual state? How does one describe a spiritual state of being? Good question. It occurs to me that I (whatever "I" means) exists within my physical body. I think, and my thoughts can make my body move and function. Of course, there are functions that I don't really think about that just happens automatically, like breathing. I have served as a hospital chaplain for many years, and I have witnessed numerous people nearing their physical life's end. When it did occur, the breath left their body.

If this breath is synonymous with spirit, then it stands to reason that when the breath leaves the body and it no longer moves because the body is dead, then perhaps it is the spirit that makes our body alive.

In the bible passage of Acts 17:28 the Apostle Paul tells those on Mars Hill, near the Acropolis, quoting from one of the Greeks ancient sources that In God we live (breathe) and move and have our being. He said this after introducing God to these Greeks who had a monument to "the unknown god."

If our breath comes from our Heavenly Source and we are made in that Divine image and likeness, which is Light, and if Jesus came to earth to bring attention to our relationship to the Light, then I submit that our earthly birth is first spiritual. In the gospel of John, the first chapter, it indicates that the Logos or the Logic or God or Word was turned toward the Light. John identifies the Word as Jesus Christ. The scriptures also indicate that God is Love. I hold up for your consideration that if our beginning was a spiritual birth and this spiritual birth was founded in God who is Love, then I submit to you that we all are the offspring of Love.

When we lose sight of Love, then we lose sight of ourselves. When others reflect anything other than Love to us, or we reflect anything other than Love to others, we are not being who we really are. We are Spirit beings. The sooner we are awakened to this reality, the sooner we will be able to live and love the way we were designed by our Heavenly Light Source. You and I are the offspring of Love. It is in this spiritual reality that we live and move and have our being. Any other notion will cause us to live beneath our privilege!

Behold the Lamb

This reflection is centered around the declaration made by John the Baptizer at the baptism of Jesus of Nazareth. This declaration was made prior to the temptations of Jesus in the wilderness. Prior to these recorded temptations, Jesus came to his cousin John the Baptizer to be baptized. Baptism is a symbol of resurrection. John is recorded to have made a proclamation that this Jesus was "The Lamb of God that takes away the sin of the world." He is recorded to have made this proclamation by inviting all that were present to "behold" him. The word "behold" simply means to observe, to look at and to see.

To behold something is to perhaps become aware of a reality that has not been recognized or considered. For the Jewish people living in Jesus' day, animal sacrifice was a normal occurrence. In the New Testament of the bible and in the book of Hebrews chapter nine and verse twenty-two, it indicates that without the shedding of blood, there is no remission of sin. The writer of Hebrews is offering an awareness of how animal sacrifice and particularly how blood played such an important role in the annual ritual of purification of the Jews. When John the Baptizer makes this proclamation concerning Jesus, in essence he is directing mankind's attention away from the status quo of animal sacrifice to behold God's Lamb.

God's Lamb was alive. Jesus came to deliver a message to the world based upon Life not death. Death had played an horrendous part in humanity's history in such a way that it had been projected on to Mother/Father God as if it was God's idea to kill even though one of the commandments specifically communicated, "Thou shall not kill."

You are invited to consider what this proclamation entails. Since Moses, the development of animal sacrifices for the remission of sin has taken on a somewhat business-like standard for those looking for purification and it continued to occur year after year. Jesus even cleared the Temple while the animals over-turned tables in their escape from becoming sacrificed, saving their lives, because a business had developed selling animals to be sacrificed. Jesus indicated that they had turned his Father's house of prayer into a den of thieves.

Consider The Lamb of God! Animal sacrifice was believed by the practicing Jews that somehow the sacrifice would appease an angry God due to the sins of mankind. Perhaps "The Lamb of God" was God's way of providing His own Lamb due to mankind's angry violent behavior. In other words, it's not an angry God that is even possible to behold, accept in our minds. Rather, it is mankind's anger that has brought about fear, mistrust and their violent behavior that ultimately causes murder. It is this hateful mindset that needed changing.

It is being suggested that The God of Love has never been angry with mankind. This may be new information for you, but consider what love includes. True love casts out fear meaning with the absence of fear becomes the only thing that matters. Trust builds relationship and relationship promotes peace. Even the birth announcement of Jesus recorded in the gospel of Luke the second chapter indicates in verse fourteen in the heavenly host's praise, "peace on earth and goodwill toward mankind."

When Jesus' disciples made comments concerning the magnificence of the Temple, Jesus tells them that the day was coming when the Temple would be destroyed. Are you aware of what ceased when the Temple in Jerusalem was destroyed in seventy AD? The priesthood no longer exists meaning that animal sacrifice has become non-existent as well. When the crucifixion of Christ occurs, the veil in the Temple that separated the Holy of Holies from the rest of the temple was torn into two pieces revealing the Holy of Holies. It was recorded that this renting of the veil occurred from top to bottom. In other words, mankind did not cause this tearing of the veil. Those managing the temple certainly would not have instigated such an occurrence.

The Holy of Holies was where Mother/Father God met with the High Priest annually for the purification of the Jews. Jesus indicated to the Samaritan women at the well, recorded in John chapter four, that the true worshippers shall worship the Father in spirit and in truth: for the Father seek such to worship the Godhead. Mother/Father God is a Spirit, and the Holy Spirit is the Divine Feminine that so often gets ignored by masculine humanity because they believe to recognize that aspect of themselves embracing the feminine would take away their so-called control. The Holy of Holies is within each of us for it was declared by the Apostle Paul that we are the temple of Mother/Father God, for the Spirit of God dwells within each of us (I Cor. 3:16). It is in the Christ energy that we breathe and move and have our being.

This brings us back around to the idea of "beholding." "To behold the Lamb of God" simply means that we have awakened to this reality because we now can see and remember it. The awareness of the result of Jesus entering our ignorant darkness bringing Mother/Father God with him by his teaching, was profoundly addressed from the Roman cross upon which he hung. "Father forgive them, for they know not what they do!" In other words, the retribution of God is not anger toward us but forgiveness. You are a daughter or son of the Most High God and Mother/Father God loves you very very much!

Behold his Face

The first time I recall seeing the image of the face of Jesus from the standpoint of a black man was when I was invited to visit an African-American pastor friend in his home. When I entered his home, I was warmly welcomed. As I began to notice pictures he and his wife had displayed on the walls of their living-room I noticed a familiar painting. It was the famous Last Supper with Jesus Christ and his disciples. As I observed closer it became apparent that all the figures in the painting were black. This encounter took place several years ago but the impression it has made on me began to help my understanding regarding the way different cultures view familiar images. So I looked on the internet to discover African-American religious art. Sure enough there was the black artist's rendition of a biblical scene with Jesus and his disciples and they were all black. As I began to search various cultures it became apparent that each culture viewed the same scene through the eyes of their own culture.

If black people recognize Jesus as being black and white people recognize Jesus as being white then its no surprise that Asian people recognize Jesus as being Asian and the Indian recognize their Jesus as being Indian. That goes for every kind of people anywhere on planet earth. The apostle Paul is recorded to say that Jesus became all things for all people. If that is the case, then I suspect that that is exactly what Jesus is to each and every one of us whether we are aware of it or not.

Here is something for us to consider. The image of Jesus observed by His disciples Peter, James and John recorded in the gospel of Matthew, chapter 17, may give some insight about our image. The Matthew account tells us that Jesus transfigured into a being of light. We are the offspring of that Light and that makes us all one In Source! When we behold the image of Mother/Father God, then what we are viewing is our own reflected image of pure Light! We are beings of reflection. We have the ability to reflect the Light of God or Source or Divinity or whatever you call it but please understand that our ability to reflect the Light of God can also cause us to reflect negative energy that is directed by those projecting fear toward us because of what has been reflected to them, thus lowering our loving vibration. We have freewill and we can decide what we will reflect. Your reflection will remain loving as long as forgiveness is part and parcel of your healing power. We are all Light reflectors so let your light so shine!

Bad Theology

In the early verses of the ninth chapter of John of the New Testament there is an interesting conversational exchange between Jesus and his disciples. This chapter deals with an outcast who was identified as being born blind. The question was asked of Jesus, "Who did sin that this man was born blind?" The questioning continued that perhaps if it was not the blind man then perhaps it was his parents. Jesus looks at his disciples and announces that neither the blind man nor his parents were to blame for his blindness but that the works of God would be revealed in him.

My reflection today centers on the idea of bad theology. I suppose bad theology often surfaces where there is no spiritual revelation. Revelation is simply removing the veil so the truth can be seen without any obstacles blocking the view. In our blind man example the disciples of Jesus operated under the notion that sickness or unfortunate circumstances was the result of sin. It is very interesting what bad theology can accomplish when it is left to its own merits. Once truth is covered over, every time the falsehood is stated, there is a reinforcement of that lie. It may be an innocent lie but a deception nonetheless.

How does one determine what is truth and what is not? How does one identify bad theology? Here is a thought for you to consider. This thought will suggest that the identification of such theological notions cannot be determined alone. What these disciples had with them at the time was Truth Incarnate. In other words, Jesus was and is the Truth. So, what he shared with them was exactly true. When he said that neither the blind man nor his parents were to blame for his blindness then resting on this revelation as truth began to break down their bad theology.

As the story continues and the blind man received his sight the works of God were revealed in him as a testimony to the Truth. I suppose the disciples of Jesus began looking at those people identified as "outcasts" differently from that point forward. There is a follow-up story in Acts chapter three that confirms the disciples' change of heart. Peter and John were going to the temple around three o'clock in the afternoon to offer prayers when they encountered a lame man seated at the temple gate. It also states that he was lame from his mother's womb.

Sounds familiar doesn't it? The blind man in John chapter nine was blind from his mother's womb. When the lame man asked for money Peter said, "Silver and gold have I none but such as I have, I give to thee. In the Name of Jesus Christ of Nazareth rise up and walk!" No longer do we hear these disciples questioning whether these so-called outcasts were in their predicament due to sin. The truth told by Jesus concerning the blind man transferred to the lame man revealing the works of God in him.

Jesus did not leave us alone after his crucifixion. As a matter of fact, he said he would send another Comforter which is the Divine Feminine we call the Spirit of Truth. The way we can discern bad theology now is by listening to the Divine Mother-God known at the Holy Spirit. Relying on man's interpretation of scripture as the final word is not recommended. That means that you should not take my word for it either. *Ask the Spirit. She will tell you the Truth!!!!*

Angels Unaware

The year was 1990. I was involved in chaplaincy training at the Baptist Medical Center in Pensacola, Florida. One of my very best friend's father was at the end of his earthly life and soon the news came that he had died. The funeral service was planned and I made the decision to go in support of my friend and his family. Sometimes events occur that carry with them a landslide of meaning. Sometimes it takes several years to sort through such meaning and while you think you have sorted through it all the realization of only scratching the surface communicates the absolute enormity of God. Such was the event that unfolded before me that day in 1990.

I traveled from Pensacola eastward along interstate highway ten to where the funeral was being held. The car I was driving was relatively new. I did not anticipate any problems to surface while making this journey. I arrived at my destination and attended the funeral service. Because of my relationship with the family of the deceased it was a special time spent together as they remembered fondly the love and care of their father and grandfather and husband. Eventually we said our goodbyes and I began to make my trip home.

I remember the funeral was on a Wednesday because along with securing my chaplaincy training, I also served as the minister of music in a local congregation. Alabama and arriving to participate in their mid-week prayer service was the next item on my agenda. I recall as I started my car there was a hint of a possible issue with my battery. It seemed to be somewhat sluggish but it did start and so off I went getting back on the interstate driving westward toward Gulf Shores. All of a sudden, the engine began to die and the car began to slow down and as a result I rolled to a stop on the shoulder of the highway. There I sat not really understanding the mechanical problems being encountered. I tried to start the car again and just like normal the car started up and I once again was headed toward my destination in Alabama. Three or four miles down the road the same thing happened and before long I was rolling to a stop on the shoulder of the highway. I tried to start the car but it appeared the battery was dead. I sat there longer thinking what I was going to do next. I tried to start the car again and wouldn't you know it the car started up like normal and once again like Willie Nelson, I was back on the road again.

I recall approaching an off ramp and thinking that perhaps I could get some assistance at a gas station but somehow my urgency to get to the church in time for the mid-week service seemed to blur my judgement and so I continued along the highway. It wasn't long before my car was once again rolling to a dead stop. This time there was no sign of life in my car and looking around it appeared I was in the middle of nowhere. I got out of the car and raised the car's hood. The events that occurred next still bring a sense of awe to me. Perhaps they will for you as well.

There I stood next to my rather new car in the middle of an area that looked like a swamp with seemingly no idea how I was going to get home let alone the mid-week prayer service at the church. It was a long walk back to the off ramp. There were no cell phones then. So here it what I did. I looked skyward and with an audible voice I said, "God! I need some help!" Within a matter of minutes two motorists stopped to help me. Of these two, one was a man in an Oldsmobile. He told the other motorist that he would take care of me so the other gentleman said, "Okay" and went on his way.

How do I describe to you how this gentleman assisted me? I explained the symptoms and he sort of scratched his head and then he jumped my car off from his car and next thing I knew I was back on the road heading for the church service. He followed me to see if my car was going to behave again as I had described. Sure enough, it did. My battery was done for so this gentleman took his battery out of his car while his engine was still running and replaced my battery with his. Soon we were back on the road. We had decided to stop at an auto parts store and I would purchase a new battery which I did. Once it was installed and he placed his battery back in to his car we were back on the road again. He told me that he had begun his trek that morning from Georgia. I don't recall him telling me where he was going. What he did say was that he would see me to the church making sure that I arrived there safely. It was getting late and sure enough we both arrived at the church just before the service began. I invited him to come and worship with us. He said he would but asked me not to draw attention to him. So in order to say thank you I sang a song of praise to God. Once the service was over he waved goodbye and that was the last time I saw him.

I have often thought about that eventful day. I can still hear the silence while being stranded on the highway pondering what to do next. My prayer to God also echoes within me. The swiftness of the answer, the confidence to carry me safely to my destination even though I had not communicated where I was headed, and all of this given by a perfect stranger in such a loving way continues to bless me to this day. Hebrews chapter thirteen verses one and two says, "Treasure family bonds and friendship. Family fondness remains the essence of this kingdom. Treat strangers with equal affection; they could be a messenger of God in disguise!

Calamities and Destructive Storms

The seriousness of this reflection cannot be downplayed. While driving to work one morning alone in my vehicle, I heard a voice in my spirit tell me to "look up! what do you see?" It is difficult to explain what it is like when such a voice speaks to you. All I can tell you is that it was undeniably plain spoken. I did not get the sense that I was being forced into anything. I just did what was being requested in that moment.

When I heard this voice back in the spring of 2017, I was baffled as to why I was chosen to hear this voice. When I looked up into the sky, I saw numerous cloud formations. One formation appeared to resemble a pair of wings. I recall saying audibly, "it looks like wings." The voice told me to find the passage on wings. When I came across Psalm 57 in the Amplified Bible that morning, it seemed to begin a quest of trying to figure out what "calamities and destructive storms" was being revealed. The first verse read,

"Be merciful and gracious to me, O God, be merciful and gracious to me for my soul takes refuge and finds shelter and confidence in You; yes, in the shadow of Your wings will I take refuge and be confident until calamities and destructive storms are passed."

At first, I thought such storms had to do with my personal life's journey. Then COVID-19 hit, and I began to consider that the pandemic must be what the voice was holding up for me to see. I think the pandemic is only part of the meaning of calamities and destructive storms. The scriptures are very plain when it indicates that the earth is the Lords and the fullness thereof, the world and they that dwell therein. The Lord God is Love! God is not angry or judgmental regarding his children, and we are all God's children. However, as God's children, we have taken it upon ourselves, due to our misunderstanding of God's nature, to believe a lie that God stands in judgement against us.

The lie we have internalized has caused us to believe that we are alienated from God and each other. This alienation is ripe with mistrust. When such mistrust continues long enough the outcome is violence and separation. If you don't believe that then you haven't been listening to current events. Just recently more and more people are speculating that the United States is on the verge of a civil war. If such a war is coming, then the arrival of such conflict is not coming from God but from our own selfish and greedy mistrust of each other. This is apparent from the haves and the have nots.

What may be lurking around the corner will catch numbers of people off guard. When people are caught off guard then their action will be retaliation. If retaliation becomes the order of the day, then violence, bloodshed and death will reign. Jesus told us that the enemy comes not but for to steal, kill and destroy. Jesus told us that he came to give life and to give it more abundantly. The only way to survive what may be lurking around the corner is to find refuge and confidence in the shadow of His Wings.

The principalities and powers of evil are real spiritual entities. They harbor fear, anger, and promote alienation from God. This alienation from God is a mindset built upon a lie. Remember, Jesus said that satan was a liar from the beginning. Jesus Christ is The Truth. He is closer to you than your next breath because of His love for you. God believes in you. You would not exist apart from God's love. When you internalize and believe the lie that God is judging you, then you join in with the enemy promoting fear and alienation from God and each other.

If the Spirit of God thought it important enough to raise awareness to find shelter and confidence under the shadow of His wings until calamities and destructive storms are passed, then I beseech each of you to at least give this possibility some prayerful thought so when things are revealed, you won't be caught off guard!

Unbelief

There is a story recorded in the Bible found in the gospel of Mark the ninth chapter that I have heard most of my life. It is the story of the man whose son had been plagued with something so severe that whatever was influencing his life it caused him to experience behaviors that from an outside observation were life threatening. As a matter of fact, these behaviors had controlled him from early in his life. When the father sought out help from Jesus' disciples to rid this child of this malady, they were unable to help.

Now prior to this encounter Jesus, Peter, James, and John were returning from the mountain where Jesus was transfigured revealing that he is the Light. When they arrived to where the other nine disciples were gathered with this father and son along with a crowd of people, Jesus asked what was going on. When he learned that these nine disciples could not help the child, Jesus seems to express his dismay at this entire faithless generation that even though he had been with these disciples for so long, they still had difficulty knowing.

This entry has to do with unbelief. I know something about unbelief. Perhaps you do too. I know that I don't like to admit the issues I have had during my life where unbelief seemed to control my actions. For this father who brought his son to find the help he needed seemed to develop a healthy sense of doubt. Now these disciples are only re-enforcing his doubts with no help surfacing for his son.

Jesus asks the father to bring his son to him. Then the child began to demonstrate the kinds of behaviors that had been so alarming to his father. Jesus asked how long this had been going on. The father replied since he was a little boy. That is when the father, with tears in his eyes, pleaded with Jesus to do something if he could. Jesus asks the father if he believed he could heal the boy. As I thought about this question, something seemed to be revealed that I had not thought of before.

Here is a man with strong and compassionate feelings of love for his son. It occurs to me the parallel process that may be being revealed here. God the Father has that kind of love for His Son Jesus. As this earthly father emotionally seeks help for his son, Jesus asks the father if he believes he can heal him.

Then the father puts forth an honest reply, "I believe. Please help my unbelief." So, what did Jesus do for that father and his son? First, he heals the son. Coupled with that healing he helps the father's unbelief.

Unbelief is something we all wrestle with from time to time. When doubt becomes so overwhelming that finding our way out of that darkness seems impossible, then we are invited to reexamine how the Light plays the essential role in our healing. When we become aware that Jesus is the Light and it is this Light that ushers in our healing, then we begin to understand the necessity of the Light and without this Light there is only darkness. Whatever your healing need is, remember that this Light is already within you because we are made of this Light!

Non Violence

This reflection concerns one of the oldest issues humans face daily. When we are threatened or made to feel as though we are going to lose something of value; when what we have worked for becomes the target of interest by others, we often find ways to return the threat to cause the original threat to go away. These kinds of tactics to protect our family or property or sense of wellbeing, have been practiced for centuries. The part that often gets overlooked however, pertains to the possible outcome when these tactics get ramped up to a level where we take the law into our own hands and usually the result is violence.

When we covet our own status or when we decide that what we have acquired is ours exclusively, particularly considering wealth, religion, race, or culture, then the lengths we will go to guard that status is to first of all become a verbal insult to the threat. If that does not bring the results we are wanting, then violent attacks may very well be the next step. The ultimate outcome of this violence is bloodshed and murder.

If we can find a way to justify our actions that alleviates the threat whether real or imagined, even if our justification is filled with hatred of others, then our behavior will be reflected to people who share our so-called status and soon they become our allies. If enough people reflect our hatred of others because we have convinced ourselves that they are the enemy, and we are convinced we are going to somehow lose our precious status, then it is almost guaranteed these intense feelings will bring about violence and murder.

As was indicated earlier, violence and murder have been a part of humankind since Cain killed his brother Able as recorded in the book of Genesis of the bible. What is being held up for the reader to consider pertains to how we can justify acts of violence and murder even though it plainly says in the ten commandments, "Thou shall not kill.;" There was an article indicating that a local minister communicated to his congregation that it was of God to take up arms against the enemy. Perhaps loving your enemy and doing good to those who despitefully use you, spoken by Jesus, was not taken into consideration.

Here is something to at least think about. If it is true that Mother/Father God is love, then God cannot hate at the same time. If Jesus is the Prince of Peace, then he can't be the Prince of war at the same time. You can't have it both ways. War, anger, and conflict originates within the imagination of mankind. When we project these kinds of thoughts onto a God of Love then we change the God of Love into a god of war, anger and conflict making this self-made god our ally. When we are convinced that we have this god on our side, then we give ourselves permission to do harm to anyone we decide is our enemy and this god justifies our actions.

Here's hoping you will consider that the God of Love is just that, Love! God is not angry with you. God loves you! God is not out to judge you or to separate you from God's presence. God loves you and Jesus the Christ energy, came to school room earth to communicate that love to us all. Experiencing hatred and anger from others is not pleasant. We have all made our share of mistakes. The conduit that brings the love of Mother/Father God to fruition is forgiveness. The proof of that is what Jesus is recorded to have said from the cross upon which he was crucified, "Father forgive them, for they know not what they do."

ibrations

Have you ever watched and listened to someone tuning a stringed musical instrument? Perhaps you have performed this exercise yourself. As each string is plucked it gives a tone based upon the number of vibrations per second. I was taught that four hundred forty vibrations per second is the agreed upon universal pitch for A. Now with all of the electronic devices at our disposal finding the correct pitch to begin the process of tuning stringed instruments is much easier.

Of course, if the vibrations either increase or decrease the human ear will hear higher or lower sound pitches. In Charles Haanel's book entitled "A Book About You" he offers the following, "When the frequency is more that 38,000 vibrations per second, the ear cannot recognize sound; when 400,000,000 (million) vibrations have been reached, we perceive the sensation of light, and as the vibrations gradually increase, the eye perceives one color after another until violet is reached with its 75,000,000,000 (billion) vibrations per second."

Wow! As I attempt to get my mind around the idea of vibrations per second and what is manifest as vibrations increase, I can't help but consider how the concept of light, spoken of in John's gospel, is somehow inter-connected with Spiritual vibrations. John describes Jesus as the Light Source and His life is the light that defines our lives. He says that the darkness was pierced and could not comprehend or diminish the Light. Usually "darkness" spoken of in John chapter one is an indicator of mankind's ignorance of their redeemed identity and innocence. In other words, to be in the dark would mean that a person couldn't see or perceive even with their eyes wide open.

In Matthew 5:16 Young's Literal Translation says, "so let your light shine before men, that they may see your good works, and may glorify your Father who is in the heavens." I know that the Light Source is already within us because we wouldn't exist apart from it. Some people cover their light over with a bushel basket and seem to retreat from the Light of our lives. Some choose darkness rather than light because their deeds are evil the scriptures say.

The good news about human lives is contained in the reality that The Light Source shines in our darkest darkness and our darkest darkness cannot overpower that Light. And this Light is within each of us.

I believe this is true and when you hear this truth, perhaps for the first time, it will begin to vibrate within you causing an awakening to the Light that too has always been within you.

The Yolk

Have you ever experienced a situation whereby you entertained a moment of inspiration and then perhaps shared it with a good friend? After you shared it, your friend gives you a look that communicates, "you just now coming to this?" I've seen this look before, I'm thinking, "so you've known this for how long and you haven't shared it with me?" I had one of those not long ago so I'm taking the chance of sharing it here in hopes that some of you will rejoice that I'm just now coming to this. But there may be those reading this reflection where maybe this will be your initial moment of inspiration. Either way as we reflect together it is amazing to me how one moment of inspiration can open a reservoir of divine influence inviting us still deeper.

In Matthew chapter eleven Jesus issues an invitation for rest to all those who labor and are heavy-laden. The word used for labor seems to mean those who are growing weary by the moment under the stress and strain of one's circumstances. Then Jesus continues the invitation by offering his yoke.

My path into chaplaincy training took place at the Baptist Medical Center in Pensacola, Florida. I was blessed to interact with several fellow pilgrims seeking similar training. One of those fellow travelers was a Catholic Priest name Jerry. He had served as a missionary in Africa. One day we were discussing the passage in Matthew related to the yoke and particularly how easy it is. He looked at me and asked if I understood what that meant. You know how some of us are when we are asked such questions, "...oh sure, I know what that means"! Truth is, I didn't know and perhaps he could sense that, so he preceded to relay his experience from his missionary days. He told me that he had observed the Africans carving out a yoke to pair up two oxen for the purpose of plowing a field. He said that the yoke would fit over the oxen's shoulder blades. If the yoke did not fit well it would begin to rub a sore place on the shoulder blade and once that happened, these animals would not pull at all. If the yoke was "easy" meant that it fit well, and the animals would pull all day.

Now I'm not sure why it has taken me this long to figure this out but for as long as I have heard this invitation to "...take my yoke upon you" in my mind's eye I saw myself taking the yoke of Jesus and putting it on my shoulders. It never occurred to me that Jesus was already in his yoke and for me to take it upon myself meant that he accompanied the invitation.

Duh! Once I got this then "learning of him" began to make sense. It's not my yoke! He doesn't need to learn of me. He already knows me better that I know myself. One of my African American students added to my understanding by informing me that often a more experienced animal is paired in the same yoke with one that is being trained. Once I visualized that I am yoked together within the yoke of Jesus Christ and this union is within me, I fell into that reservoir I spoke of earlier.

The way we think is vitally important to the way we are! I want to encourage you to begin seeing yourself yoked with the Christ energy that Jesus came to reveal. No matter what your circumstances, visualize within yourself taking every step you take initiated by the one whose yoke you wear!

The Revelation

What this reflection will hopefully reveal is based on questions we may ask ourselves we did not know that were lurking beneath the surface of our theological understandings. Our awareness of these questions, often come from the Spirit of Jesus or the Christ energy of Mother/Father God. With such questions lurking beneath the surface, please be reminded that Jesus hid some of the most amazing truths in plain sight while those so-called listeners walked away scratching their heads in dismay.

The Apostle Paul's letter to the Galatians starting with verse eleven and ending at verse seventeen is as follows in the New King James Version.

But I make known to you, brethren, that the gospel which was preached by me is not according to man.
For I neither received it from man, nor was I taught it, but it came through the revelation of Jesus Christ.
For you have heard of my former conduct in Judaism, how I persecuted the church of God beyond measure and tried to destroy it.
And I advanced in Judaism beyond many of my contemporaries in my own nation, being more exceedingly zealous for the traditions of my fathers.
But when it pleased God, who separated me from my mother's womb and called me through His grace,
To reveal His Son in me, that I might preach Him among the Gentiles, I did not immediately confer with flesh and blood,
Nor did I go up to Jerusalem to those who were apostles before me; but I went to Arabia and returned to Damascus.

Considering this passage, one may become curious concerning the Damascus Road experience of Saul of Tarsus. It is recorded in Acts chapter nine. Saul, who became known as Paul the Apostle, never met Jesus in the flesh. The Jesus Saul met on the road to Damascus was a blinding Light. This Light was so spiritually bright that it physically blinded him for the next three days. When Saul asked who it was that was speaking to him the reply was, "I'm Jesus whom you are persecuting."

Seeking to control others is very masculine with no evidence of the Divine Feminine. Having traditions that control you may be something worth giving some additional thought to moving forward. So now Saul sets out for Damascus with orders from the higher-ups in the temple in Jerusalem, of which Saul secured, to persecute those who now follow the teachings of the Christ energy. Then suddenly, he experiences something he was not anticipating.

Having the "control rug" pulled out from under Saul had to have been a paradoxical moment. Think about it. If the only way we will be able to spiritually see is to recognize our blindness (John 9) then it makes total sense that the Light that blinded him for three days became the Light that would guide him for the rest of his life. It might occur to us that most of the theological beliefs espoused from preachers and teachers who received them from preachers and teachers, kind of like Saul, quickly changed once Truth was spiritually revealed in an unexpected situation.

What this reflection seeks to hold up for the reader to consider is based on the significance of what was written in Galatians chapter one. Paul indicates that the gospel (good news) that he proclaimed did not come from man nor was it a message from which he was taught. This good news was The Revelation of the Christ energy he experienced on his memorable journey to Damascus. It was not "a" revelation of Jesus, rather it was the heart of Mother/Father God within the Christ energy being revealed to Saul in pure Light. Within that revelation all kinds of Truth came pouring out to him. Saul had a complete one-hundred and eighty degree turn around that was so spiritually earth shattering that now even his name changed from Saul to Paul. It is very interesting to note that Paul did not go directly to Jerusalem to look up those who had known Jesus in the flesh but rather based on such an intense spiritual encounter, Saul needed to encounter this Christ energy in the Divine Feminine of Holy Spirit, so he spends three years in Arabia before returning to Damascus.

Paul even shares an amazing understanding that this Jesus he encountered on the Damascus Road was already within him. It cannot be stressed enough the importance of "revelation."

As one continues their spiritual journey, consider being open to the Revelation of the Christ energy and the Truth that comes from Mother/Father God that already dwells within everyone. Make the decision to ask The Spirit before you decide to follow the teachings of man. There is a lot of that kind of stuff out there. In asking the Spirit first, you will continue to discover, amid this Revelation, a Relationship that is second to none. So, the question to ask is simply, "whose revelation are you considering?" Don't take my word for it! Ask the Spirit, she will help you!

The Light Seed

When was the last time you looked at an oak tree, I mean really looked at one? Depending on the height of the tree or how big around its trunk is may give some indication as to how long the tree has been in existence. At one point this mighty oak tree was a small seemingly insignificant acorn. You can pick up an acorn from off of the ground and toss it back down again never really giving any thought to the potential that lies within it. Nor do we usually give much if any thought to the amount of time necessary for the potential within the acorn to become that mighty oak tree that you have witnessed many times. Most of the time we only think about the part of the oak tree that we see above the ground. However, within that acorn is also the potential root system that serves as the tree's foundation that also sustains it with nutrients. When you think about it, the acorn, though very small, is a tremendously significant and essential part that makes the oak tree what it is.

Please keep in mind the picture of the oak tree as this reflection continues giving thought to a different kind of seed that too needed time to germinate and grow. In the Genesis account of creation written in the first couple of chapters in the bible, it is recorded that God said, "Let there be light." The light spoken of here is not the sun. According to the creation story, the sun came into being on the fourth day of creation. Our sun is a star and there are now billions upon billions of stars throughout the universe but what is being held up for consideration is the possibility of what was planted, so to speak, when the "big bang" occurred billions of years ago that science held as theory but recently is now embracing as fact.

What if the light that Mother/Father God spoke into being was the seed potential that when given enough time to germinate, sprout and grow would in essence be the universe that is still unfolding. Our physical bodies are made up of various elements that come from the stars that have exploded at the end of their life cycle sending out into space their remnants. Without those elements, our human bodies would not be made like they are. At the time of the universe's beginning, stars did not exist, but their potential was present. With regard to the oak tree, the same is true that the oak tree's trunk did not exist when the acorn was first introduced into the soil but the potential was very present.

The idea that humanity is made in the image and likeness of Mother/Father God that said, "Let there be light" is an indication that we are light beings. Master Jesus, just like the rest of us, contains the Christ energy that is depicted by our heavenly Light Source. We all are made from this Light. As the universe continues to unfold so do we. Our potential that came from the Light Seed planted billions of years ago continues to reflect within each of us. As the vibrations continue to heighten within us, we continue to become brighter light reflectors for the spiritual benefit of all to aid in their spiritual journey. There is no telling how many times we have journeyed on school-room earth to bring us to where we are today. Just like the oak tree, its beginning from a seemingly insignificant acorn to eventually becoming a majestic oak tree would not exist without the Light.

This Light dwells within each one of us. Not only does this Light dwell within us, but we are also made from this Light. We are becoming and will continue to discover the various possibilities that will surface as this Light Seed continues to grow. The potential is set free by imagination. So let your Light so shine before everyone and in so doing they will glorify the one that said, "Let there be light!"

Believing is Seeing

A number of my recent thoughts are concerned with the idea of seeing. On the surface the notion of seeing may be thought of as a matter of fact. One may say, "Of course I can see. Can't everyone?" The point I am hoping to convey here relates to the idea that to think one can see brings with it a certain blindness. In other words, to grasp the reality of what is really happening in a given situation only surfaces with an awareness of one's own blindness. I suppose an example would be helpful at this point.

Jesus is recorded to say that he is the light of the world and that in him there is no darkness at all. Jesus indicated to Peter that on the knowledge that He, Jesus was the Rock on which His church would be built and the gates of "hades" would not prevail against it is very significant. Hades means "not to see." The church built on Jesus Christ would be able to see spiritually. This spiritual sight does not come in the form of self-confidence. Rather, this sight only surfaces in humility. Here's another example.

Jesus is nailed to a Roman cross and is placed between two thieves. At some point as they hung there a conversation ensued between them. One thief says to Jesus, "If you are the Son of God get us and yourself down from here." The other thief responded to his cohort, "Don't you fear God seeing we are in the same condemnation?" Then addressing Christ, the second thief says to Jesus, "Remember me when you enter into your kingdom."

As we consider this conversation it is important to perhaps "see" what the second thief saw that caused him to reply to his thief companion. What do you think he saw in Jesus? They were all being tortured to death. What would make him say, "Remember me when you enter into your kingdom?" Just because Jesus was being crucified did not snuff out or extinguish the fact that He was the Light of the world. What Jesus says to this thief completely relates to the idea of seeing.

Jesus proclaims, "Truly I say unto you, today you will be with me in paradise." I was not aware of the meaning of this statement until just recently. The word "paradise" means to see up close! Do you understand what Jesus was telling this man? Allow me to paraphrased it for you.

"Now that you have had your eyes opened in that you have recognized me from where you hang on your cross, the distance between us is now removed and from now on you will see me up close. So up close, in fact, that my peace will flood your soul and so thrill you as you bask in the Light of my presence in you and even death cannot separate us."

Paradise does not begin when one transitions from the physical world through death. Paradise is experienced the moment our eyes are opened and we see the Christ for who he really is, our Savior and Redeemer. That seeing is never at a distance. That seeing is always "up close." If you have never experienced this paradise, I urge you to investigate until you find it!

This edition published 2025
Copyright @ 2025 by Alan Carden
www.bridgebuilder101.com